THE SPORT SCIENCE HANDBOOK

THE SPORT SCIENCE HANDBOOK

A BLUEPRINT FOR BETTER DECISION-MAKING IN SPORT

ADAM VIRGILE | MARC LEWIS

Printed in the United States of America.

First Edition

ISBN: 979-8-218-70337-0

For permissions or inquiries, please contact:
sportscinetwork@gmail.com

The Sport Science Network
sportsciencenetwork.com

CONTENTS

WHAT THIS HANDBOOK IS (AND ISN'T)

This handbook is a compass for navigating the messy, complex world of applied sport science. It won't give you a step-by-step map, but it will keep you pointed in the right direction: improving performance while reducing injury risk.

We focus on the thinking patterns and foundational principles, the **Big Rocks**, that matter most, no matter your setting. Whether you're working with Olympians or high school athletes, backed by a big budget or flying solo with a whiteboard, these Big Rocks can help you practice more effectively.

You will not find exhaustive physiology reviews or equipment manuals here. Those resources already exist. This handbook teaches you something more fundamental: how to think clearly about complex problems and implement simple solutions that actually work.

HOW TO USE THIS HANDBOOK

This handbook is designed as a practical guide and quick-reference tool for applied sport science. Throughout the book, you'll find icons that highlight takeaways, mental models, foundational principles, and practitioner perspectives to help you focus on what matters most in your context.

Each chapter builds upon the last to form a complete framework for effective sport science practice. However, the chapters can also be used individually when tackling specific challenges.

As you read, resist the urge to implement everything at once. Start with one principle, apply it fully in your environment, and build from there. Practitioners who try to overhaul everything at once usually end up changing nothing sustainably.

Above all, this handbook is built for action, not just understanding. You'll find decision frameworks, implementation tools, and real-world examples throughout because sport science only creates value when it is applied in the unpredictable and demanding reality of competitive sport.

Your situation may differ from the examples we share. Your constraints, athletes, resources, and organizational dynamics are unique. The six **Big Rocks** (see Introduction) remain constant, but how you apply them will depend on your context. This handbook gives you the raw materials, not a rigid blueprint, for building your own sport science system.

ICON KEY

ICON	LABEL	MEANING
	Key Takeaways	Summarizes the most important points for quick review.
	Mental Model Moment	Highlights essential thinking frameworks for effective practice.
	Big Rocks	Foundational principles to prioritize before adding complexity.
	Practitioner Perspective	Real-world insights and advice from experienced professionals.
	Applied Integration	Targeted exercises designed to turn chapter concepts into action.

INTRODUCTION

THE $1 MILLION QUESTION

"If you don't have time to do it right, when will you have time to do it over?"

JOHN WOODEN

IF YOU HAD $1 MILLION to improve athletic performance, what would you buy?

We asked hundreds of coaches, and the answers are remarkably consistent. Most coaches said they would invest in force plates, GPS systems, heart rate monitors, altitude chambers, and advanced camera systems: expensive technology that promises to unlock hidden performance potential.

Here is what 20 years of applied sport science practice have taught us: the million-dollar answer isn't found in any equipment catalog. High-performing sport science teams we've encountered often operate with modest budgets, while organizations with unlimited resources sometimes struggle to turn technology into better decisions. The difference is how practitioners think about problems (**Figure 1**). Effective sport scientists use the same tools differently because they think differently.

Consider two wrestling programs. The first owned a $10,000 force plate system that sat untouched in the corner of the equipment room. The technology was flawless, but using it required athletes to arrive 30 minutes early for testing, which conflicted with team meetings. The analysis software was so specialized that only one staff member could operate it. When that person was unavailable, testing stopped. Worst of all, the data never influenced coaching decisions.

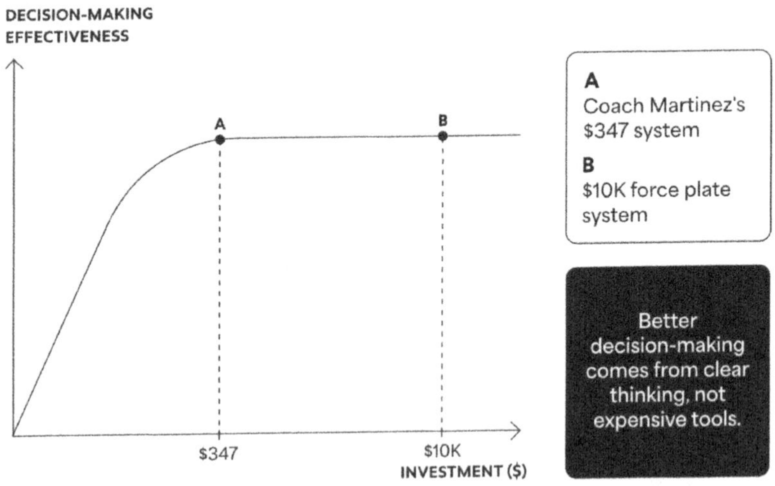

Figure 1. *Financial investment vs. decision-making effectiveness: Higher spending on technology doesn't guarantee better sport science outcomes or improved decision-making capabilities.*

Meanwhile, 200 miles away, Coach Martinez revolutionized his high school wrestling program's weight management using only $347 worth of equipment: a digital scale, a smartphone app, and a whiteboard. Each morning, athletes recorded their weight and energy levels. The information automatically updated a shared dashboard that Coach

Martinez reviewed over breakfast. Simple rules triggered immediate responses: if weight dropped too fast or energy levels fell dramatically, he modified training activities, added nutritional support, or temporarily restricted competition participation until the trend stabilized.

That approach was simple, consistent, and directly tied to daily decisions that affected health and performance. It ran smoothly for three years and eliminated unsafe weight-cutting practices. The lesson was never about equipment. It was about fit. The system worked because it aligned with real-world routines and decisions instead of relying on complex tools that didn't. Technology doesn't drive progress. Clarity does.

The Big Rocks Principle

In sport science, it's easy to get buried under data, devices, and dashboards. Many practitioners start with the latest tools and methods, then wonder why their systems still feel disjointed. The problem usually isn't effort or intelligence. It's order.

Stephen Covey illustrated this idea with a simple demonstration. He filled a jar with large rocks until no more fit and asked, "Is the jar full?" The audience said yes. He then poured in pebbles, sand, and finally water, each filling the gaps the rocks left behind.

"The lesson," Covey explained, "is that if you don't put the big rocks in first, they will never fit."

In sport science, we often do the opposite. We fill our jars with technology, data, and complex methods, then wonder why there's no space left for the things that truly matter **(Figure 2)**.

Over the years, we've learned that every effective sport science system, no matter the sport, resources, or technology, shares a few essential foundations. We call them the six Big Rocks. They're not the only things that matter, but they're the things that matter first. Focus on the six Big Rocks, and everything else will start to make sense.

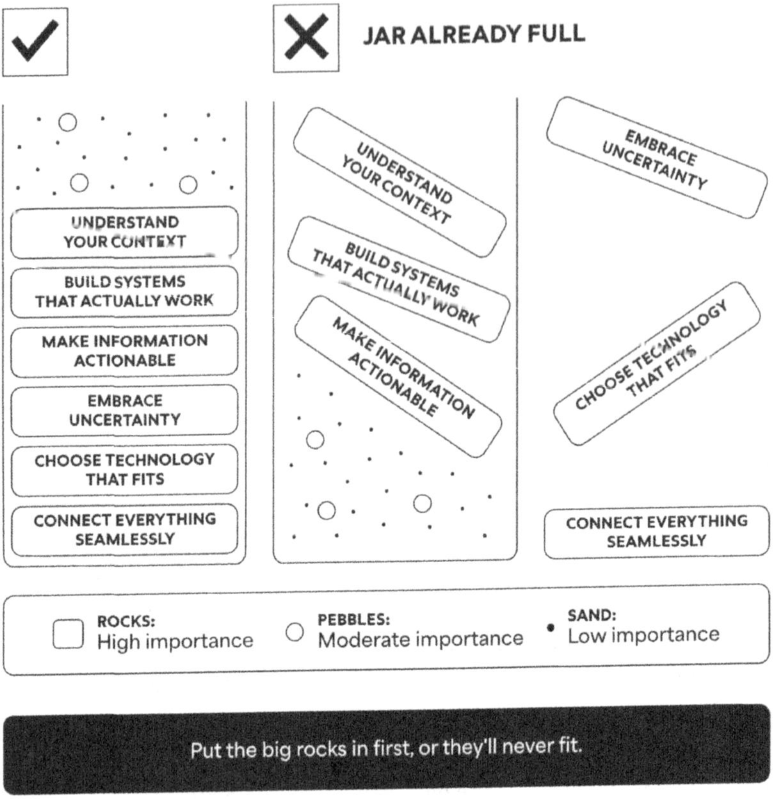

JAR ALREADY FULL

UNDERSTAND YOUR CONTEXT
BUILD SYSTEMS THAT ACTUALLY WORK
MAKE INFORMATION ACTIONABLE
EMBRACE UNCERTAINTY
CHOOSE TECHNOLOGY THAT FITS
CONNECT EVERYTHING SEAMLESSLY

ROCKS: High importance
PEBBLES: Moderate importance
SAND: Low importance

Put the big rocks in first, or they'll never fit.

Figure 2. *Big Rocks principle: Fundamental sport science principles must be established first, or smaller tactical elements will crowd out what matters most for effective practice.*

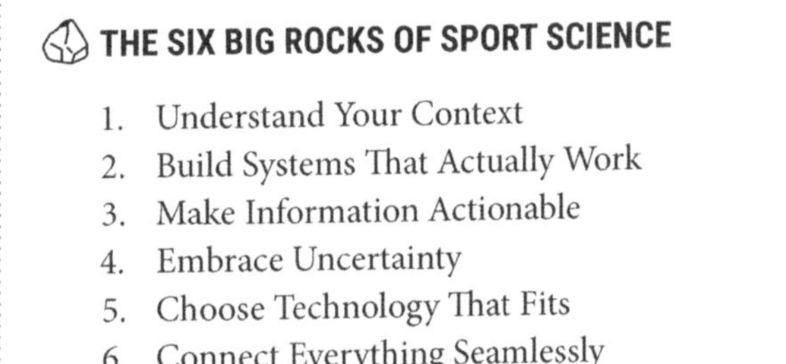

THE SIX BIG ROCKS OF SPORT SCIENCE

1. Understand Your Context
2. Build Systems That Actually Work
3. Make Information Actionable
4. Embrace Uncertainty
5. Choose Technology That Fits
6. Connect Everything Seamlessly

These are not just categories on a list. They describe how effective practitioners think and operate. You can strengthen any one for immediate benefit, but mastering all six creates a multiplier effect. Instead of asking, "What is the most advanced technology we can buy?" savvy practitioners ask, "What is the simplest solution that solves our most important problem?" Think of your system like packing a suitcase. Put the most important items in first and fit everything else around them. You can't always take everything you want, but in sport science, make sure the essentials—the six Big Rocks—are the things that stay in the bag.

The Mental Models Difference

Throughout this handbook, we will explore how certain thinking patterns, or mental models, separate effective practitioners from those who struggle despite having access to the same resources and information.

Mental models are frameworks for understanding how things work. They help you recognize patterns, anticipate consequences, and make decisions under uncertainty. A swimming coach once told us, "Learning to think probabilistically changed everything. I stopped saying 'this athlete is overtrained' and started saying 'this athlete shows increased risk of overtraining.' That one shift led to better conversations and better outcomes."

These thinking tools are not abstract concepts, but practical frameworks used daily by experienced practitioners. They help you navigate the gap between textbook knowledge and real-world application, between having data and making good decisions.

Consider an athlete whose jump performance declines for three consecutive days. One practitioner cuts training. Another considers measurement error, motivation, or technique changes. A third compares patterns across other athletes before drawing conclusions.

Same data, completely different approaches based on different thinking patterns. The practitioner using more sophisticated mental models will consistently make better decisions, regardless of the technology available. Better mental models beat better equipment. Every time.

Handbook Focus

The seven chapters ahead will transform how you approach sport science challenges. We'll begin by defining the foundational principles that underpin effective practice, then explore each of the six Big Rocks in depth. By the end, you'll have gained more than just knowledge, you'll have developed the thinking patterns that drive consistent success in sport science and decision-making.

The journey starts with a simple truth: the most powerful tool in sport science isn't found in any catalog. It's the ability to think clearly about complex problems and implement simple, consistent solutions. Master the fundamentals, and everything else falls into place. Ignore them, and even the most advanced tools become expensive paperweights.

Focus relentlessly on fundamentals that create the foundation for everything else.

 KEY TAKEAWAYS

INTRODUCTION

- Master the six Big Rocks before adding complexity.
- Use clear, consistent thinking to make better decisions in any environment.
- Build solutions that fit your unique context instead of copying others.

1

SPORT SCIENCE FUNDAMENTALS

"Get the fundamentals down and the level of everything you do will rise."

MICHAEL JORDAN

SPORT SCIENCE PRESENTS A PARADOX: it's both simple and complex. Our goals, improving health and performance, sound straightforward, yet achieving them requires navigating a web of physiology, biomechanics, psychology, motor learning, and environmental factors. These elements interact in ways we are still uncovering, especially when working with teams rather than individuals.

What Is Sport Science?

The National Strength and Conditioning Association (NSCA) defines sport science as "the application of scientific processes to improve athletic and team performance and decrease the risk of injury." This definition highlights two core elements that guide practice.

First, performance enhancement and injury prevention are deeply interconnected, not separate goals. Athletes can't perform at their best when injured, and pushing too hard or preparing poorly often increases injury risk. This relationship grows more complex in team environments, where one athlete's injury can affect entire tactical systems and collective performance.

Second, sport science is rooted in the scientific process: making observations, testing hypotheses, gathering data, analyzing patterns, and refining methods based on evidence. Importantly, "scientific" doesn't mean complex or high-tech. Often, the most scientific approach is the simplest one that reliably answers your questions and improves your decisions.

Sport science encompasses multiple interrelated domains:

- **Biomechanics**: Movement patterns and force generation
- **Physiology**: Training response and metabolic adaptations
- **Psychology**: Mental factors affecting performance
- **Nutrition**: Fueling strategies and dietary optimization
- **Recovery**: Managing fatigue and restoration processes
- **Training methodology**: Program design and periodization
- **Performance analysis**: Collecting, analyzing, and communicating performance data
- **Load management**: Balancing stress and recovery

These domains function as a deeply intertwined system where changes in one area ripple through all others (Figure 3). Improving one element inevitably influences the rest of the performance ecosystem. Even a simple goal like jumping higher involves multiple layers working together: building stronger muscles (physiology), perfecting technique (biomechanics), focusing attention (psychology), and ensuring sufficient energy (nutrition and recovery). Adjust one element, and the rest must adapt. The value of sport science lies not in its individual parts, but in how well they work together.

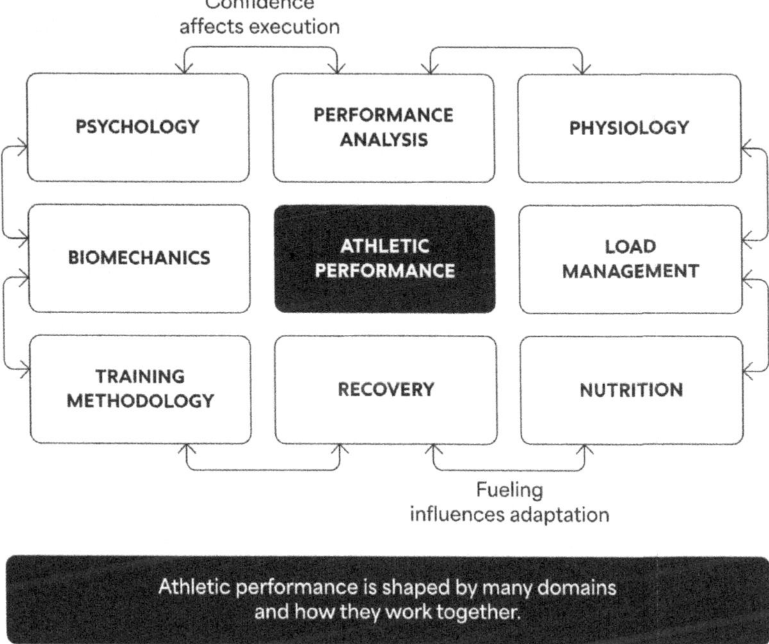

Figure 3. *Interconnected sport science domains: Multiple specialized areas work together as a connected system where changes in one domain affect athletic performance outcomes across all others.*

In team sports, everything becomes more complex. A soccer team might include a striker who needs explosive power training, a goalkeeper recovering from a shoulder injury, and midfielders managing different fatigue levels—all while the coach needs the team to execute the same tactical system. You're constantly balancing individual optimization with collective performance.

The Reality of Individual Variation

Here's a truth that textbooks and research papers often overlook or gloss over: each athlete is their own case study. Even identical training programs produce vastly different outcomes across athletes. The same athlete can also respond differently to identical stimuli at different points in time (**Figure 4**).

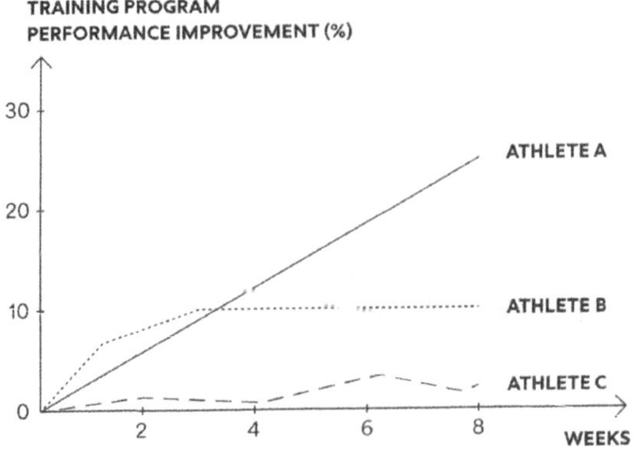

Every athlete is unique. Even identical training programs produce vastly different responses in different athletes. Even the same athlete responds differently to identical stimuli at different times.

Figure 4. *Individual training responses: Three athletes following identical programs show vastly different performance improvements, illustrating the inherent variability in biological adaptation.*

This individual variation (what researchers call the "N=1 problem") is both the greatest challenge and the most fascinating aspect of applied sport science. While general principles and averages are valuable, the athlete standing in front of you today may respond completely differently than expected based on previous experience or research literature. This is why we can't simply copy successful programs. What works perfectly for one athlete or team may fail entirely for another.

Consider a soccer team implementing a new conditioning protocol. Some players might show rapid improvements in endurance, others might adapt slowly, and a few might regress before improving again. These differences stem from factors such as training history, stress levels, sleep quality, and genetics. This variability isn't a flaw in your program. It's biology. Effective practitioners expect it, plan for it, and adapt to it. They build flexibility into their systems and learn to recognize when individual adjustments are needed. The goal isn't to eliminate individual variation but to manage it skillfully. That ability often separates good practitioners from great ones.

This natural variability is why sport science can't depend on rigid templates. Systems built on fixed rules often fail in dynamic situations. What endures are clear principles that help you make sound decisions even when conditions shift. That's where systematic thinking begins.

Why Systematic Thinking Matters

Given the complexity and variability of human performance, how do we make consistent progress? The answer lies in systematic thinking: developing frameworks that help you navigate complexity without becoming overwhelmed by it.

Systematic thinking doesn't mean rigidly following procedures. It means having clear principles that guide decisions while maintaining flexibility in how those principles are applied. It's like understanding driving principles rather than memorizing specific routes. When you understand the fundamentals, you can navigate any road, even when conditions change.

Mental models are the foundation of systematic thinking. They're cognitive frameworks that help with:

- **Pattern Recognition**: Spotting what matters in messy data
- **Decision Architecture**: Breaking down complex choices into manageable steps
- **Uncertainty Navigation**: Making sound decisions without perfect information
- **Context Adaptation**: Adapting principles intelligently across different situations and environments
- **Learning Acceleration**: Drawing lessons from both successes and failures

Throughout this handbook, you'll encounter specific mental models that experienced practitioners use daily. These are not academic theories; they're practical tools that immediately sharpen your effectiveness. Systematic thinking turns complexity into clarity. It transforms uncertainty into informed action.

The Team Environment Challenge

Team sports introduce unique challenges that individual athlete work rarely encounters. Understanding these complexities is essential for anyone working in group settings.

Scale Complexity: Managing twenty to thirty athletes simultaneously requires different systems than working with individuals. Methods that work perfectly for three athletes often collapse under the scale of a full roster.

Diverse Needs: Team members differ in position demands, injury history, training age, and physical readiness. A monitoring system that captures a defender's readiness might overlook crucial information about a goalkeeper's recovery.

Multiple Stakeholders: Coaches, medical staff, strength coaches, analysts, administrators, and athletes all have unique priorities and communication styles. A report that satisfies one group might not be helpful for another.

Dynamic Contexts: Team environments shift constantly with injuries, competition schedules, tactical adjustments, and roster changes. Your systems must adapt while maintaining consistent principles.

Social Dynamics: Individual optimization can sometimes clash with team cohesion. The strategy that maximizes one player's performance might disrupt chemistry or tactical balance. For example, a basketball team may rest its star player before playoffs, but doing so could hurt team rhythm and confidence.

These challenges are not obstacles to eliminate. They're realities to understand and work within. Individual athlete work is complicated. Team sport work is exponentially more complex. High-level practitioners don't resist this complexity. Rather, they build systems designed for it. Success in team environments depends less on controlling complexity and more on learning to navigate it.

Common Failure Modes in Sport Science

Recognizing how sport science programs fail helps you avoid predictable pitfalls. Most breakdowns follow familiar patterns.

Technology-First Thinking: Starting with impressive tools rather than clear problems. This creates sophisticated systems that rarely improve decisions or outcomes.

Data Collection Without Purpose: Gathering information simply because you can rather than because you need it for a specific decision. The result is overwhelming information and cluttered dashboards that paralyze rather than clarify.

Context Mismatch: Copying approaches that work elsewhere without adapting to your unique setting, resources, and constraints.

Stakeholder Disconnect: Building systems that make sense to you but not to the coaches, athletes, or medical staff who depend on them.

Complexity Overload: Attempting to monitor everything at once instead of starting simple and expanding based on proven value.

Perfection Paralysis: Waiting for ideal conditions or complete certainty before acting. In high-performance sport, hesitation can cost more than imperfect action.

Communication Breakdown: Producing insights that are technically correct but presented in ways that fail to drive action.

Recognizing these patterns allows you to course-correct quickly when they appear. But the best strategy is prevention. Start with a clear purpose. What problem are you solving? How will information influence decisions? When you can answer those questions confidently, most failure modes never appear. Programs that fail often start with solutions and search for problems. Programs that succeed start with problems and design solutions **(Figure 5)**.

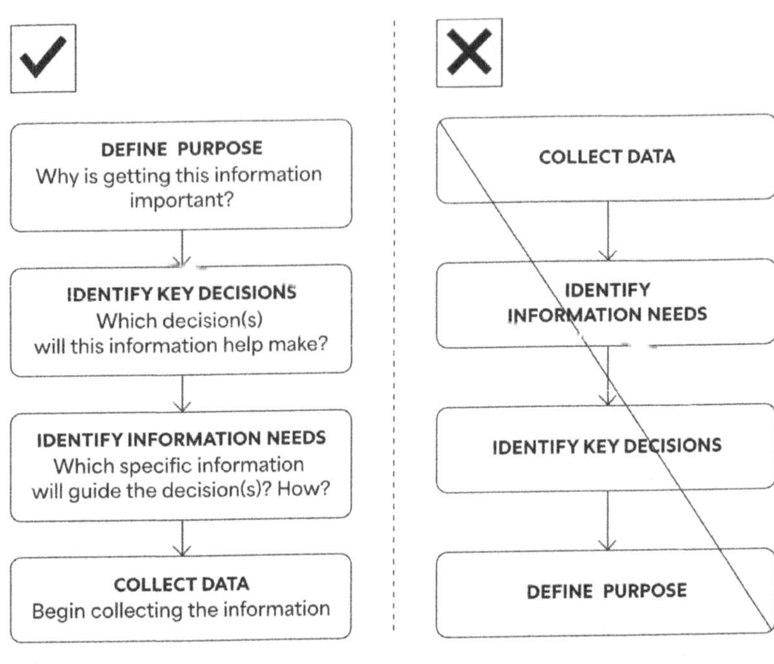

Figure 5. *Purpose-driven workflow: Starting with clear problems and decisions leads to meaningful data collection, while starting with data collection often results in irrelevant information gathering.*

The Scientific Method in Applied Settings

In applied sport settings, scientific thinking is less about running perfect experiments and it's more about approaching problems with structure and humility. The same principles that guide laboratory research can be adapted to daily practice if they are simplified and focused on decision-making.

- **Observation**: Notice patterns in athlete performance, response, or outcomes that warrant investigation.
- **Question Formation**: Develop specific, answerable questions about what you observe.
- **Form Predictions**: Form testable ideas about what may be causing the pattern or how interventions might help.
- **Test Your Ideas**: Implement small, controlled changes to evaluate your predictions while maintaining athlete health and performance goals.
- **Data Collection**: Gather information systematically to asses whether your predictions were correct.
- **Analysis and Reflection**: Interpret results honestly, including unexpected or negative findings.
- **Iteration**: Refine your approach based on what you learn and repeat the process.

The value of this process is found in its repeatability. It transforms trial and error into structured learning, helping practitioners make evidence-informed decisions without requiring laboratory control or complex statistics.

PRACTITIONER PERSPECTIVE

Q: What three to five tips would you give sport scientists for crafting clear questions that ultimately inform decision-making?

MATT JORDAN, PhD

"I learned a valuable lesson early on. It is all about achieving the desired training effect and accumulating better training responses while minimizing the occurrence of worse training responses. Little things add up and doing the simple things extremely well backed with quality training is what it is all about. This is the main driver for why we monitor. It isn't about injury or performance prediction although I know as a profession, we will continue to push this envelope. It is about getting a little better each day with our preparation.

To keep it simple, and drive a better framework for incorporating a data-driven approach, answer these few questions:

1. What is my training hypothesis for the upcoming phase? This should be something like by focusing on the training stimulus 'x' I expect the training response 'y' to occur.
2. What was the training load in the previous week or micro cycle?
3. What is the athlete's context in the current phase? Where will they be located, what is going on in their personal life, how are they feeling about their progress?
4. How are they doing from a medical and health standpoint?
5. How are they doing from a training standpoint?
6. Are there any red or yellow flags that you need to be aware of?

At the start, your answers to these questions may be subjective and opinion based. But see if you can begin to create one or two metrics for each question that might help to counterbalance the risk of confirmation bias or illuminate something you have missed. Keep it simple, start with the easy things to measure and the ones that you and your athlete can be consistent on.

For example, maybe you'll use a weekly countermovement jump to track jump performance and leg power output, and you'll quantify the expected training load with your own sessional rating of perceived exertion (sRPE) and duration. Maybe you'll add in a measure of resting heart rate and heart rate variability with a wearable or a couple of daily wellness questions. But the important thing is to start answering those six questions each week before you prep for the upcoming week. You may find that you naturally start finding metrics to support your opinions and observations. The process of becoming more data-driven isn't about collecting more data or making it fancy. Prediction is complex but preparation is simple. Accumulating better training responses and minimizing the accrual of worse training responses is what it is all about."

► **MATT JORDAN**
Player Health & Performance Scientist and Faculty of Kinesiology at Sport Medicine Centre | University of Calgary

The scientific process in applied sport science doesn't require lab conditions nor advanced statistics. It requires curiosity, systematic observation, and honest evaluation of outcomes.

For example, a volleyball coach notices players seem unusually fatigued on Tuesdays. Instead of accepting this as normal, she applies scientific thinking: she observes the trend, hypothesizes that Monday's training may be too intense, adjusts the session, tracks Tuesday fatigue, and evaluates the results. This mindset, involving structured observation, hypothesis testing, and evidence-based adjustment, separates effective practitioners from those who rely solely on intuition or tradition, doing things a certain way simply because they always have.

Building Your Foundation

This scientific mindset leads to several foundational principles that guide effective practice.

- **Start Simple:** Complex problems often have straightforward solutions. Begin with the basics before adding sophistication.
- **Focus on Decisions:** Make sure that every piece of information connects to a specific action you take.
- **Expect Iteration:** Your first approach won't be perfect, and that's fine. Improvement comes from refinement, not perfection.
- **Respect Context:** Solutions must align with your environment and constraints. What works elsewhere can inspire you, but it can't instruct you.
- **Communicate Clearly:** Insights only create value when they reach the right people at the right time in usable form.
- **Plan for Variability:** Individual differences and changing circumstances are constants to work with, not problems to eliminate.

These principles provide stability and direction while allowing the flexibility needed to adapt to your specific situation. They guide everything that follows in this handbook. Master these foundations, and the rest becomes easier. Ignore them, and nothing else works.

PRACTITIONER PERSPECTIVE

Q: What advice would you give to sport scientists overwhelmed by too much information to help them clearly identify what actually matters?

SAM CONTORNO, MS

"In a world of technological abundance, it is important to understand that more data doesn't necessarily lead to better decision-making. Technology and data should be incorporated based on a department's need, rather than the latest trend. The three questions to consider for whether technology and data implementation is worth it are as follows:

1. ***Is the data accurate?*** *Does it compare to the gold standard? Does it solve a departmental problem? Does it test or train an adaptation that positively drives sport performance?*
2. ***Is the data efficient?*** *Can you logistically test your roster and turn around the data in enough time to influence decision-making?*
3. ***Is the data actionable?*** *Are there collaborative department interventions to address deficiencies discovered from testing?"*

► SAM CONTORNO

Associate Director of Applied Sport Science |
University of Texas at Austin

EMMA BEANLAND, MS

"With the rapid emergence of new technologies in the sport science domain, practitioners must ensure the collection of valid and reliable data or refrain from collecting altogether. Data should serve to inform decision-making, initiate meaningful conversations, and provide actionable insights into athlete performance across a range of stakeholders.

The selection of screening protocols or physical assessments should begin by asking the right questions, setting the foundation for determining what truly matters. A structured workflow I apply when navigating large volumes of data begins with clearly defining the key questions: what are the goals of the assessment, and does the proposed technology support investigating them? Followed by a literature review to identify gold standard practices, understand methodological limitations, and account for sources of error and potential confounding variables. The final step involves reporting only valid and reliable metrics, supported by appropriate statistical analysis to ensure meaningful interpretation.

Practitioners must be intentional when selecting assessments and seek opportunities to integrate data sources for deeper insight. For example, combining force plate countermovement jump (CMJ) and single limb countermovement jump (SLCMJ) metrics with physical therapy orthopedic screenings can reveal deeper athlete movement signatures. To enhance athlete and coach engagement, present reference comparisons that contextualize current performance to previous assessments, rolling averages (e.g., last five or ten sessions), lowest and all-time best historical values or positional benchmarks. These comparisons help ground feedback in relevance and clarity. The decision to adopt a specific technology should also consider the time, resources, energy, and relationship impact on both athletes and staff. In practice, successful implementation often involves embedding assessments into training environments, creating a seamless integration where testing becomes a natural extension of performance monitoring.

Finally, and perhaps most importantly, ensure that data interpretation creates a positive feedback loop. While statistical rigor is essential, the communication of findings must be accessible and coach-friendly, allowing for actionable insights that foster trust and buy-in across the performance team."

▶ **EMMA BEANLAND**

Applied Sports Scientist | Buffalo Bills

The Path from Fundamentals to Practice

These fundamentals prepare you to apply the six Big Rocks systematically. Each builds on these principles and provides a framework for real-world decisions.

So far, you have seen what sport science is, why individual responses vary, how systematic thinking manages complexity, and the unique demands of team environments. But principles alone are not enough. The effectiveness of any approach depends on how well it fits the people, culture, and constraints of your environment. That's why the first Big Rock is **Understanding Your Context**. Before measuring, monitoring, or optimizing, you must understand your setting. The best practitioners don't have the most advanced tools. They have the clearest understanding of what matters in their environment.

Effective sport science applies systematic thinking to complex, variable environments. It builds on sound principles, adapts to changing realities, and connects every insight back to meaningful action.

 KEY TAKEAWAYS

SPORT SCIENCE FUNDAMENTALS

- Sport science improves performance and reduces injury risk through integrated, systematic thinking.
- Individual variation requires flexible, context-aware approaches.
- Strong fundamentals provide stability in complex, evolving environments.

2

UNDERSTANDING YOUR CONTEXT

"Culture eats strategy for breakfast."

PETER DRUCKER

BIG ROCK #1

Understanding Your Context

REMEMBER COACH MARTINEZ from the Introduction? While one college wrestling program's $10,000 force plate system gathered dust, his $347 setup that included a scale, a whiteboard, and a shared dashboard quietly eliminated dangerous weight-cutting practices.

That contrast wasn't about money or technology. It was about alignment. The first program had impressive tools, but they didn't match the practical realities of athlete schedules, staffing, or daily decision-making. Coach Martinez's solution aligned with his environment, which is why it worked and why it lasted.

That's the essence of our first Big Rock: **Understanding Your Context**. Before implementing any sport science approach, you need a clear picture of your environment, resources, constraints, and stakeholders. Even the most advanced tools fail when they ignore the realities of the setting they serve.

The Context Reality Check

It's important to remember that an approach that succeeds brilliantly in one situation may fail completely in another. The difference isn't the quality of the science; it's how well the science fits where it's applied.

Context isn't a limitation; it's a strategic advantage. When you understand your environment deeply and design solutions that work within it, you create systems that others can't easily copy. Your specific combination of resources, culture, and operations becomes the foundation for approaches that belong only to you.

Think about two teachers. One has thirty students, limited time, and basic supplies. The other has fifteen students, flexible scheduling, and ample resources. Both can create excellent learning outcomes, but their methods must match their realities. The first may rely on group activities and peer learning, while the second can focus on individual projects and personal feedback. Neither is superior; each is optimized for its own context.

Sport scientists need the same mindset. Don't try to recreate someone else's setting. Excel within your own. Just as a teacher adapts methods to their classroom, effective sport science means adapting your techniques to your situation rather than forcing your environment to match ideal methods.

The Four Dimensions of Context

To effectively understand your context, examine four key dimensions that shape every decision you make.

1. *Resource Context*

Write down exactly what you have. Use real numbers, not wishful thinking. How many hours per week can you devote to sport science? What is your budget for tools and technology? Who can help collect, analyze, or act on data? What spaces and equipment are consistently available?

A high-resource program might have dedicated staff, substantial budgets, and advanced facilities. A low-resource program might rely on one coach wearing multiple hats, with limited funds and shared spaces. Both can be effective, but their systems must reflect their resource realities.

Be brutally honest about time. If you have two hours per week, don't design systems that require significant daily upkeep. If your budget is small, avoid plans centered on expensive tools. If you're the only operator, build redundancy or keep it simple.

2. *Cultural Context*

Culture determines how information is received and acted upon. Observe what already works. Do coaches prefer quick talks or detailed reports? Do athletes respond better to group or individual feedback? Do administrators emphasize safety, performance, or both?

Build around existing cultural patterns instead of fighting them. If coaches make training decisions in hallway conversations, integrate insights there. If athletes are skeptical of technology, begin with simple approaches that demonstrate value before adding complexity.

Culture also includes communication preferences, leadership dynamics, and organizational hierarchy. A military academy, a liberal arts college, and a professional club all function differently. Even two programs with identical structures can operate in opposite ways depending on personalities and relationships. Match your message to the people, and your ideas will move.

3. *Competitive Context*

Ask what performance margins matter most. A one-percent improvement can determine medals for Olympians but means little for youth athletes.

Consider timing as well. Professional teams competing every few days need different monitoring than college teams playing weekly. Developmental athletes require broad-based improvements, while elite athletes refine details. Understanding competitive context helps you aim effort where it changes outcomes rather than where it only changes numbers.

4. *Operational Context*

How are decisions made in your setting? When do coaches plan sessions? Where do athletes receive feedback? How does information move between staff? The formal organizational chart rarely reflects the real workflow.

Map when and where key choices occur. A professional basketball performance staff discovered that the real moment of practice planning happened during the brief huddle the coaches held ten minutes before practice. When the staff sent their readiness reports the night before, the suggestions rarely showed up in the next day's plan. Once they began sharing concise insights right before or during that huddle, the information finally influenced what happened on the court.

Operational context includes scheduling constraints, facility limitations, technology access, and communication channels. A team that travels frequently needs different systems than one with consistent facilities. Athletes balancing academics require different timing than professionals with open schedules.

These four dimensions must shape your approach **(Figure 6)**. Generic best practices aren't enough.

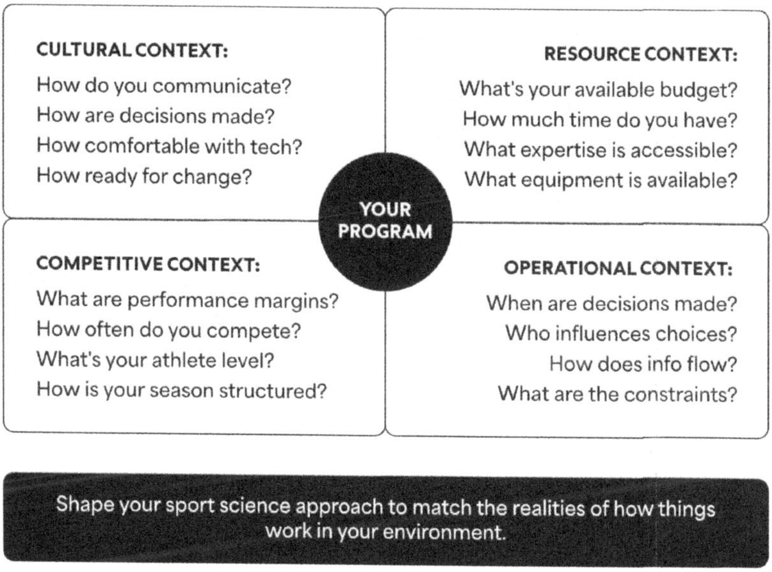

CULTURAL CONTEXT:
How do you communicate?
How are decisions made?
How comfortable with tech?
How ready for change?

RESOURCE CONTEXT:
What's your available budget?
How much time do you have?
What expertise is accessible?
What equipment is available?

YOUR PROGRAM

COMPETITIVE CONTEXT:
What are performance margins?
How often do you compete?
What's your athlete level?
How is your season structured?

OPERATIONAL CONTEXT:
When are decisions made?
Who influences choices?
How does info flow?
What are the constraints?

Shape your sport science approach to match the realities of how things work in your environment.

Figure 6. *Contextual assessment framework: Four key dimensions (cultural, resource, competitive, and operational) that must be understood for effective sport science approaches for any environment.*

Defining Decisions Before Collecting Data

Many new sport scientists start with the wrong question: "What data should we collect?" when they should be asking, "What decisions do we need to make?" This reversal leads to impressive dashboards full of unused information.

A tennis academy once struggled under the weight of data coaches couldn't use effectively. They tracked everything: stroke metrics, fitness test scores, and match stats, but none of it guided action. Coaches felt overwhelmed instead of informed. Before adding more systems, we asked three simple questions:

1. What specific decisions will this information help us make?
2. When will we need this information to make those decisions?
3. How will our choices change because of it?

That exercise revealed the truth: the academy didn't need more data; it needed clarity. Coaches simply needed a quick way to determine whether athletes were ready to train fully, needed modification, or shouldn't train at all. We replaced complexity with a simple traffic-light system*:

- Green: Full training
- Yellow: Modified training needed
- Red: Can't train today

Each morning, players submitted basic readiness inputs, and the medical team added their observations. This approach worked because it drove immediate action, improved communication, and aligned with existing routines. Everyone understood what the information meant and what to do next.

---

* *Note: Red–green color blindness can affect up to ~8% of men and ~0.5% of women, with prevalence varying by ethnicity. When possible, consider pairing color cues with icons, text labels, or alternative color schemes (e.g., red–blue) to improve accessibility.*

THE THREE-QUESTION TEST

Use this test to prevent data hoarding and keep your monitoring purposeful. Before collecting any information, you must be able to answer:

1. What specific decision will this inform?
2. Who needs this information?
3. By when must it be available?

Teams that apply this test collect less data but make far better use of it. If a metric doesn't change a decision or spark a new conversation, it doesn't belong in your system.

Context Assessment in Action

Context assessment shapes how systems perform across environments. The goal isn't to copy what others do, but to make your system fit the realities of your setting.

High School Basketball Program

Resources: One coach, $200 budget, shared gym, ninety minutes of daily practice, and fifteen players with varying skill levels.

Culture: The coach prefers simple, direct communication. Athletes respond best to visual feedback. Parents care most about safety. Administrators emphasize academics first.

Competition: Long term development is more important than single-game results. Basic conditioning and injury prevention take priority over marginal performance gains.

Operations: Decisions happen on the court in real time. There's little room for analysis between sessions. Information must be clear and immediately useful.

Solution: Short wellness check-ins during warm-up, smartphone jump testing twice weekly, and basic load tracking using perceived exertion scales. The approach worked because it was quick, practical, and aligned with daily routines.

Professional Soccer Team

Resources: Dedicated sport science staff, large budget, elite facilities, full-time athletes, and international travel.

Culture: Data-informed decision-making is expected. Players are comfortable with technology, and each stakeholder group needs information in a different format.

Competition: Small improvements make the difference between winning and losing. Game-to-game readiness must balance individual optimization with team tactics.

Operations: Multiple daily decision points, tight travel schedules, and cross-department communication require fast, automated processes.

Solution: Integrated monitoring combining performance testing, wellness tracking, and training load analysis. Automated alerts highlighted concerning patterns, and tailored reports provided the right information to the right people at the right time.

Both programs succeeded because their systems were built around their specific realities, not borrowed methods. Cost doesn't determine effectiveness **(Figure 7)**. Fit does.

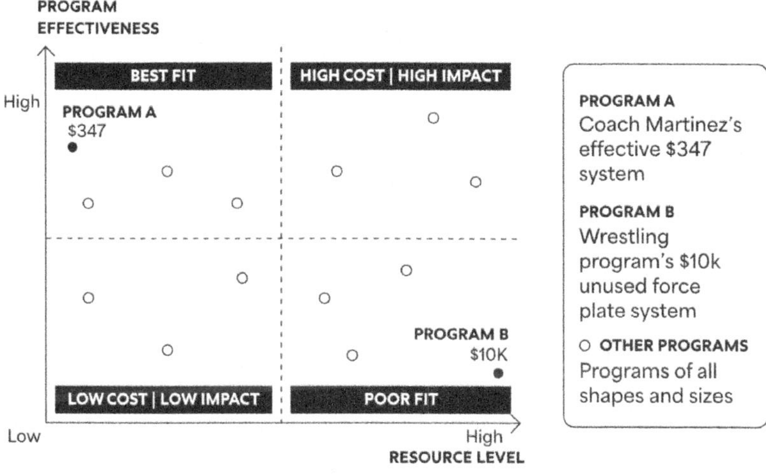

The most successful programs don't cost the most – they fit best and guide better decisions within their unique environment.

Figure 7. *Cost vs. effectiveness analysis: Programs that fit their context (like Coach Martinez's $347 system) achieve high impact regardless of cost, while poor context fit leads to low effectiveness despite high investment.*

MENTAL MODEL MOMENT

FIRST PRINCIPLES THINKING

Key Principle: Break things down to foundational truths and build up from there. Ignore assumptions and defaults.

The tennis academy's breakthrough came from first-principles thinking. Instead of assuming they needed more data because other programs collected it, they defined the real problem: "We want coaches to make better daily training decisions." Then they asked, "What is the most direct path to that outcome given our constraints?" The answer was communication, not measurement. The solution emerged from their context, not from copying others.

First principles thinking in sport science means **(Figure 8)**:

- **Start with the fundamental goal:** What outcome are you trying to achieve?
- **Question assumptions:** Why do you think you need what others are using?
- **Work backward from decisions:** What would change if you had perfect information?
- **Build up from constraints:** Given your reality, what is the simplest path to improvement?

The best solutions grow from your context, not someone else's blueprint.

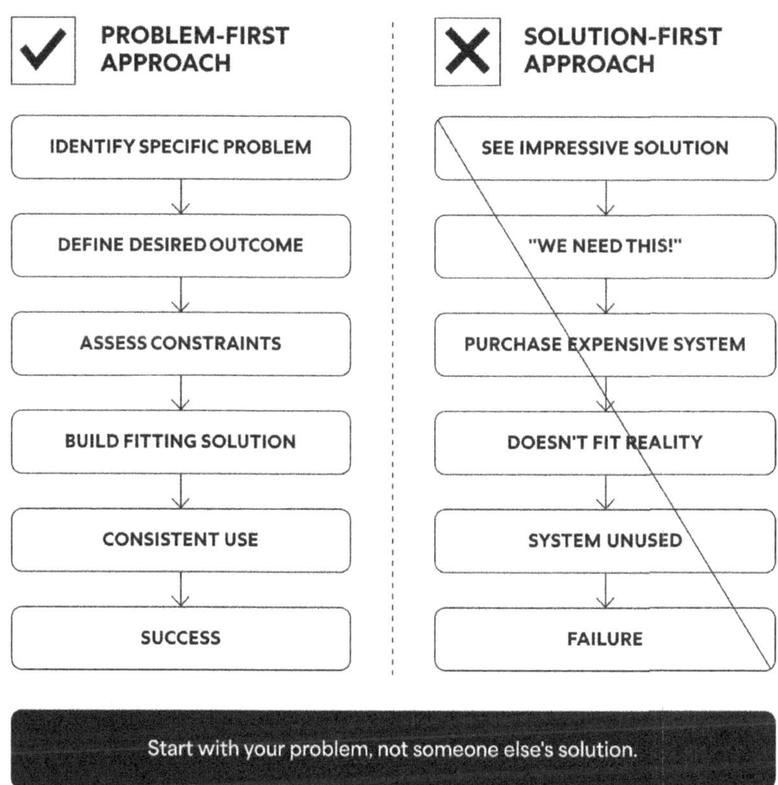

Figure 8. *First principles thinking: Starting with specific problems and building solutions from foundational constraints leads to effective outcomes, while copying impressive solutions often results in poor context fit and failure.*

Context-Aware Decision Making

Understanding context transforms how you design, communicate, and act.

1. *Information Complexity*

High-resource context: Detailed analysis, layered visuals, and comprehensive reporting are sustainable because staff have time and expertise to process them.

Limited-resource context: Simple, immediately actionable insights are essential because decision-makers lack time for deep interpretation.

Adaptive approach: Match information complexity to processing capacity. A traffic-light summary may be perfect for busy coaches, while full analytics serve dedicated analysts or advanced practitioners.

2. *Technology Selection*

Stable environment: Systems that require consistent setup, dedicated operators, and regular maintenance can thrive.

Dynamic environment: Portable, robust, easy-to-operate tools are more reliable across changing conditions.

Adaptive approach: Choose technology that succeeds in your operational reality rather than fighting against it.

3. *Stakeholder Engagement*

Data-positive culture: You can probably introduce sophisticated monitoring and expect engagement with detailed insights.

Skeptical culture: Begin with clear wins and simple approaches that prove value before adding complexity.

Adaptive approach: Build trust through early, visible impact.

Building Context-Aware Foundations

Before applying specific methods in later chapters, anchor to these principles:

- **Clarity beats complexity:** Design for your audience's comprehension and decision needs. What is clear to exercise physiologists may confuse high school athletes.
- **Context changes:** Off-season solutions may fail during competition periods. Veteran needs may differ significantly from rookie needs. Reassess regularly.
- **Communication must fit culture:** Some teams want detailed reports, others want dashboards, others prefer brief conversations. Match the medium to the people.

These principles shape everything that follows. Every tool and technique must be filtered through your context. The goal isn't to implement everything possible. The goal is to understand principles deeply enough to design solutions that hold up in your real world.

📝 Your Context Assessment Action Plan

Ready to assess your own context? Here's a practical four-week plan to get started. The aim is to build awareness, identify quick wins, and create momentum.

Week 1: Resource Reality Check (30 minutes)

Complete this assessment with brutal honesty:

- Hours per week available for sport science: ___
- Annual budget for tools and tech: ___
- Number of people who can help collect data: ___
- Consistent facility and equipment access: ___

Week 2: Cultural Investigation (30 minutes + ongoing)

Observe and document:

- How do coaches currently make training decisions?
- How do athletes prefer to receive feedback?
- What concerns do administrators raise most often?
- Who influences decisions in your organization?

Week 3: Decision Mapping (45 minutes)

For three important and recurring decisions, note:

- What information do you use now?
- When do you need to decide?
- How would better information change what you do?

Week 4: Quick Win Identification (20 minutes)

Based on your assessment, identify:

- One decision you could improve with simple information.
- One communication method that matches your culture.
- One resource constraint you can work around creatively.

Common Context Assessment Mistakes

Context assessment only works if you avoid common traps. Use this list to spot blind spots early.

- **Wishful thinking**: Designing for resources you wish you had rather than what you have.
- **Culture fighting**: Forcing people to change how they work instead of enhancing existing patterns.
- **Context copying**: Assuming what works elsewhere will work for you without considering differences.
- **Static assessment**: Treating context as fixed despite changes in people, resources, and schedules.
- **Surface-level analysis**: Focusing on obvious constraints while missing deeper cultural and operational realities.

Treat context as alive. When you adapt with it, your system stays relevant and resilient.

The Competitive Advantage

Understanding your context transforms it from a perceived limitation to a competitive advantage. When you pair awareness with disciplined decision-making, constraints become design parameters and your environment becomes the foundation for approaches others can't easily copy.

Consider the wrestling programs from the opening example. The expensive force-plate system could be purchased by any program. Coach Martinez's integrated weight-management approach grew from his specific reality: his culture, his athletes, and his constraints. Others couldn't simply replicate it because it was built for his world.

Top-notch programs rarely depend on the most advanced tools. They rely on a deep understanding of their setting and the skill to design systems that thrive within it. Start with a thorough assessment. Filter decisions through your operating realities. Build from constraints rather than resisting them. This foundation makes everything that follows not only possible but effective.

Understanding your environment turns it from a burden into a durable advantage. It enables consistent improvement, meaningful action, and sustainable practice.

In the next chapter, we'll explore how to build systems that embody this awareness and function reliably in your specific setting.

Effective sport science starts with honest assessment of your environment and constraints.

 KEY TAKEAWAYS

UNDERSTANDING YOUR CONTEXT

- Honestly assess resources, culture, competition, and operations to shape decisions.
- Define decisions first to ensure data collection is purposeful and effective.
- Treat your unique context as an advantage for building sustainable solutions.

3

BUILD SYSTEMS THAT ACTUALLY WORK

"A system doesn't have to be complicated to be effective. It just has to be aligned with the decision-making process."

DEAN BENTON

Build Systems That Actually Work

EVERY SPORT SCIENTIST EVENTUALLY ENCOUNTERS the same problem: too much information, not enough structure. Systems are what turn good ideas into lasting impact. Without them, even the best insights fade once the season starts.

Sarah worked for a basketball team with limited resources. No force plates. No GPS tracking. Not even basic heart rate monitors. Yet she had something far more valuable: a clear understanding of what mattered most for her players and the discipline to create systems that fit the culture of her program. She noticed her team struggled with fatigue during tournament weekends, particularly when playing multiple games in a single day. Instead of worrying about what she lacked, she built a basic and practical system anchored by four elements:

- A 30-second morning readiness check about sleep and soreness
- Three sprints during warm-up measured with a smartphone app
- Session RPE (sRPE)** and duration after each practice and game
- Basic performance stats from existing game footage

The strength of her system wasn't in the metrics themselves but in how she connected them. She built a straightforward spreadsheet that flagged players needing workload adjustments based on:

- Two consecutive nights of poor sleep
- Higher-than-normal sprint times
- Higher-than-normal sRPE scores
- Increased recent playing time

The system wasn't perfect, but it worked. It blended into daily routines, required minimal effort, provided clear guidance, and remained consistent. Her players stayed healthy and ready when it mattered most.

This is the essence of our second Big Rock: **Build Systems That Actually Work**. Sarah didn't begin with complex tools. She began with her environment, identified her key decisions, and built a structure that delivered the right information at the right time. Her success extended directly from Chapter 2. She understood her context first, then designed a system that fit her constraints and needs.

*** sRPE (session Rating of Perceived Exertion) is a simple, subjective rating of how hard a session felt, usually recorded on Borg's CR-10 (0–10) or 0–100 scale. sRPE Training Load, which shows strong correlations with objective load measures, is calculated by multiplying this rating by session duration in minutes.*

The Anatomy of Effective Systems

Sarah's success wasn't accidental. It followed three principles that distinguish systems that drive action from those that gather dust.

1. *Start with the End in Mind*

Before collecting any data, answer:

- What decision will this inform?
- When do I need this information to act?
- What will we change based on it?

If you can't answer clearly, you're likely collecting data for its own sake. Change one decision or metric at a time. Keep it if outcomes improve, and revert quickly if they don't.

2. *Make it Sustainable*

The best system isn't the most comprehensive one. It's the one that's used consistently. Consider who must be involved, what happens when key people are absent, and how quickly information can be processed and applied. Ask whether a new staff member could run the system next week. Ask whether it still functions when a few players have missing data.

3. *Build in Flexibility*

Plan for problems before they happen:

- What will you do if a tool stops working?
- What will you do if you can't collect the planned information?
- What will you do when your current information is insufficient to guide a decision?

PRACTITIONER PERSPECTIVE

Q: What is the most important lesson you have learned about creating structured systems in sport science that stay effective and sustainable over time?

HARJIV SINGH, PhD

"The most important lesson I've learned is that the best systems are not rigid. They're adaptive frameworks that can evolve with context, personnel, and different priorities. Early in my career, I thought 'robust' meant tightly controlled. But in practice, over-engineered systems often break under the weight of real-world complexity. It is important to build around core principles such as clarity, feedback loops, and minimal viable structure. Then layer flexibility on top. This makes the system resilient to change, not resistant to it. Sustainability emerges when the people using the system feel ownership and understand the 'why' behind it."

▶ HARJIV SINGH

Senior Performance and Development Scientist,
Basketball Operations | Charlotte Hornets

Why Systems Fail (And How to Prevent It)

A professional rugby club tracked nearly everything. Thirty GPS metrics. Daily wellness scores. Weekly strength tests. Multiple recovery biomarkers. The problem wasn't the technology. It was the paralysis it created.

When sprint speeds suggested players were fresh but wellness scores showed fatigue, which data should coaches trust? When GPS data indicated high training loads but jump tests looked normal, should they reduce intensity? Every metric told a different story. Coaches spent hours debating instead of deciding. Analysis replaced action.

The problem wasn't resistance to data. It was an excess of information delivered too late and without clear decision rules. We helped the club strip back to what mattered most: three GPS metrics (high-speed running distance, sprint count, high-intensity decelerations), three daily wellness questions, and weekly jump tests. That left ten key data points instead of fifty. Wellness provided primary context for injury-risk discussions, GPS data guided training volume and intensity adjustments, and jump tests helped confirm readiness trends and shape strength-training blocks. Defined rules replaced endless discussion, and coaches began using the system daily because it supported action rather than complicating it.

MENTAL MODEL MOMENT

HANLON'S RAZOR

Key Principle: Don't attribute to malice what can be explained by ignorance, error, or oversight.

The rugby coaches weren't ignoring data out of spite; they were drowning in conflicting metrics. Once simplified, the system worked because it fit their routines. In another case, a volleyball coach seemed to resist athlete monitoring, but the reality was that the system disrupted warm-up structures she had refined over years. Always look at the design before blaming people **(Figure 9)**.

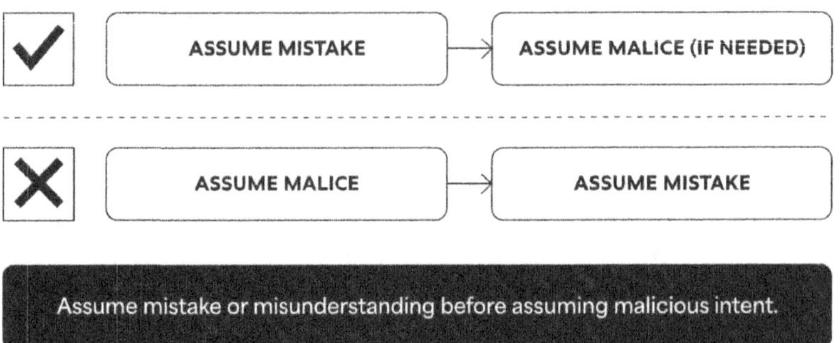

Figure 9. *Hanlon's Razor: When problems occur, assume mistakes or misunderstandings first, then consider malicious intent only if necessary—this leads to better problem-solving and relationships.*

The broader lesson is simple: in sport science, less is often more. The minimum effective dose principle means collecting the least amount of data needed to improve decision quality, not the maximum amount your technology can provide.

The Three Golden Rules

We've looked at why systems fail and how to design them better. To make these lessons stick, here are three simple rules you can apply anywhere.

Rule 1: *If you can't explain it to a high school athlete, it's too complicated*

We once watched a sport scientist explain his complex monitoring system to a college basketball team. Within two minutes of medical terminology, half the players had checked out and the other half looked confused. The approach was brilliant in theory but failed because nobody understood it.

Compare that to a team's practice board labeling sessions as Hard, Moderate, or Light, each tied to a clear duration band. Hard meant 90–120 minutes. Moderate meant 60–90 minutes. Light meant under 60 minutes. Coaches could see the plan in seconds and adjust accordingly.

Rule 2: If it doesn't fit into daily operations, it won't last

Well-designed systems enhance existing routines rather than create new ones. A college football team once tried implementing comprehensive morning assessments requiring players to arrive twenty minutes early. It lasted three weeks before scheduling conflicts with coaches brought it to an end.

Meanwhile, a high school soccer team integrated monitoring successfully by having players complete brief wellness checks on phones while changing into practice gear in the locker room, something they were already doing. The system succeeded because it enhanced routines instead of disrupting them.

Rule 3: If you're not using data, stop collecting it

Here's a basic audit. For each data point you collect, ask: (1) When did it last change a decision? (2) What would happen if we stopped collecting it? (3) Who else looks at it regularly? If you can't answer confidently, it may be time to simplify. The best systems balance usefulness with simplicity **(Figure 10)**.

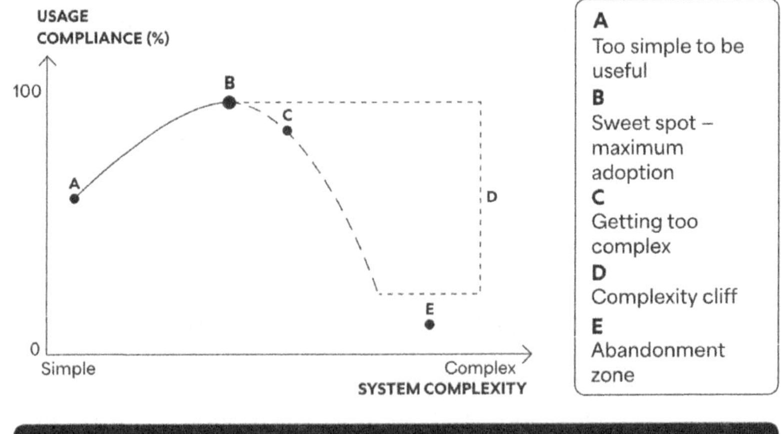

Figure 10. *Complexity vs. adoption curve: Systems achieve maximum adoption when they hit the sweet spot—complex enough to provide value but simple enough for consistent use by busy practitioners.*

THE MONTHLY SYSTEM AUDIT

A quick monthly check keeps systems lean and useful. Use these questions to decide what stays, what changes, and what stops. Ask four questions about each metric:

1. When did this last change a decision?
2. What would happen if we stopped collecting it?
3. Who besides me uses this data?
4. What action will we stop this month because the data didn't change a decision?

Teams that review systems regularly report fewer unused metrics and clearer decision-making. The goal is to track decisions that change, not dashboards that look impressive.

PRACTITIONER PERSPECTIVE

Q: What are two to three common mistakes sport scientists make when building structured routines or workflows, and how would you recommend avoiding them?

DAVE TENNEY, PhD

"There are several mistakes I commonly see in young sport science practitioners as they move into new roles in professional or collegiate sports. When getting started, they often move too quickly into wanting to provide analysis and trying to affect decision-making before establishing a proper data structure. I often use the analogy that one needs to 'build the road' (the database) before you can 'drive the car' (analysis). Once a well-structured database is in place, and good data is collected on the backend, you can then focus on creating a high-quality frontend. Good systems and routines start with a good backend development.

Second, it is critical for sport scientists to consistently review how effective their workflows are at providing actionable data that impacts the daily decision-making of the coaching staff. I often abide by an 80/20 rule: at the end of every season, I try to eliminate 20% of what we are looking at as a department in our athlete management system (AMS) daily. This process often leads to shifts in the technologies we choose and what we ultimately use.

Lastly, I often remind young sport scientists that their workflows need to be set up not just to answer their own questions but, more importantly, to answer the questions that the coaching staff has daily. Too often, sport scientists design their workflows to mainly answer their own questions from incoming data. Time and care should be taken to guide a coaching staff into asking the 'right' questions. This often requires the sports scientist to go on a journey with the coaches—helping to generate curiosity and ultimately ensuring they're asking the 'right' question."

▶ **DAVE TENNEY**

High Performance Director | Atlanta United FC

Building for Sustainability

The difference between frameworks that last and those that fade lies in how they handle inevitable real-world challenges.

Start Small and Build Trust

One of the biggest mistakes is trying to implement everything at once. It's like eating a whole pizza in one bite: possible in theory, disastrous in practice.

A college ice hockey program wanted comprehensive monitoring: training loads, recovery metrics, skating performance, physiological markers, psychological state, nutrition habits, and sleep patterns. Instead of trying to cover everything at once, they started with just sRPE (post-session perceived exertion scores).

By focusing on doing one thing exceptionally well, athletes consistently reported scores, coaches reviewed the data, patterns emerged, and trust developed. Only then did they start tracking on-ice duration. Months later, they incorporated LPS (local positioning system, an indoor GPS) for external load assessment. Like building with blocks, each new layer was added only after the previous one fit perfectly.

This approach builds confidence through early wins while avoiding the overwhelm that derails ambitious systems.

Get Stakeholder Buy-In

Convincing people to change routines requires showing clear value to each group involved:

- **Athletes**: "This helps you perform better and recover faster."
- **Coaches**: "This helps you make better decisions about training and competition."
- **Performance staff**: "This helps prevent injuries and optimize treatment."
- **Administrators**: "This protects our investment in athlete development."

Notice how none involve "because the sport scientist said so." Each group must see benefits that matter specifically to them.

Show Value Quickly

People buy into what works. A women's volleyball team implemented simple fatigue monitoring that identified three players needing modified training during crucial matches. All three stayed healthy and performed well through playoffs, while several opposing players suffered fatigue-related injuries. The immediate, visible success built trust that lasted the entire season.

MENTAL MODEL MOMENT

OCCAM'S RAZOR

Key Principle: All else being equal, the simplest explanation or solution is usually best.

Recall the rugby team from earlier in this chapter. At first, they collected nearly fifty metrics that conflicted and slowed decisions. When they simplified to just ten key data points with clear decision rules, the system finally worked. Their turnaround is a classic example of Occam's Razor: the simplest effective solution was the best one **(Figure 11)**.

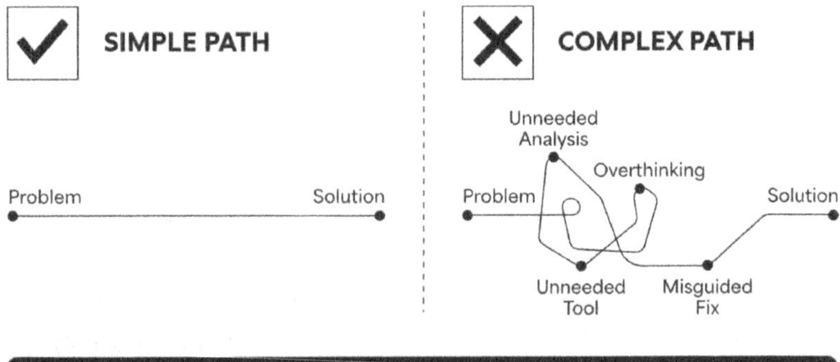

Figure 11. *Occam's Razor: Simple, direct approaches to problems are typically more effective than complex solutions with multiple unnecessary steps.*

System Design Framework

Good systems are not built in a day. Start with one decision, create the simplest version that can inform it, and keep only what proves useful. This framework helps you do that without adding clutter.

Phase 1: Purpose Definition (Week 1)

Identify your core decision: Choose one decision you make regularly that could be improved with better information. Examples include daily training adjustments, weekly strength program planning, or competition-preparedness assessment.

Apply the **Three-Question Test:**

- What specific decision will this inform?
- Who needs this information?
- By when must it be available?

Define success metrics: How will you know if your system is working? Examples: "Coaches modify training based on alerts 80 percent of the time" or "Athletes report that the approach helps them understand their competition preparedness."

Phase 2: Minimum Viable System (Week 2)

Choose the simplest approach: What is the least complex method that could inform your decision? Often, this involves combining existing observations with one new measurement.

Design collection method: How will you gather information consistently? Consider timing, location, who is responsible, and backup collection plans.

Create action protocols: Decide what happens when you receive different types of information. Write down specific responses:

- "If an athlete reports poor sleep, soreness above 7/10, and jump height down more than 5 percent, reduce training intensity by 20 percent."
- "If an athlete has not sprinted above 90 percent of maximum speed in the past three days and a game is within the next three days, add two to three maximal 40-meter sprints during practice."

Phase 3: Test and Refine (Weeks 3–4)

Run your system for two weeks. Document what works and what doesn't. Gather feedback from stakeholders: *Is this helping you decide more effectively? Is it too complicated or too basic? What would make it more useful?* Then, make one improvement. Resist the urge to change everything at once.

Phase 4: Stabilize and Expand (Month 2)

Once your core structure runs smoothly for a month, it is stable enough to consider additions. Add one complementary metric or expand to one new decision. Document your protocols, backup plans, and lessons learned for future use.

Scaling Across Contexts

The same principles can succeed in very different environments if you adapt them. What works in a professional team with many resources can also work in a high school program with fewer tools, as long as the focus remains on the decision rather than the equipment.

High School Program Example:

- **Resources**: Limited budget, shared facilities, volunteer help.
- **System**: Smartphone-based jump testing, short athlete self-report questionnaires, and coach observations.
- **Success factors**: Fits resource constraints, requires minimal time, leverages existing relationships.

Professional Program Example:

- **Resources**: Dedicated staff, significant budget, advanced facilities.
- **System**: Comprehensive GPS monitoring, detailed biomechanics assessment, and advanced recovery protocols.
- **Success factors**: Matches available resources, supports complex decision-making, enables competitive advantages.

Both work because they match the approach to context rather than forcing inappropriate solutions into unsuitable environments.

Seasonal Adaptation

A good framework evolves with the competitive calendar. Pre-season requires detail, the in-season phase demands focus, and playoff periods benefit from simplicity. Adjusting by season keeps systems useful.

Pre-season: Detailed monitoring to establish baselines and target development areas.

Competition season: Streamlined metrics that sustain insight without adding burden.

Playoff and Championship period: Minimalist focus on critical alerts and emergency-only performance tests.

A rugby team followed this approach: comprehensive monitoring in pre-season, essential metrics in season, and critical alerts only during congested match periods. Smart scaling delivered the right information to the right people at the right time.

System Maintenance

Even good systems drift if ignored. Regular, light-touch reviews keep them aligned with reality.

Consistency over perfection: A track-and-field program wasn't perfect at collecting daily soreness scores, but it was consistent enough to reveal useful trends. Perfect becomes the enemy of good, and the destroyer of sustainable systems.

Evolution, not revolution: Systems should progress through small updates, not complete overhauls. When a cricket program acquired new technology, it ran both old and new systems side by side for a month to validate methods and maintain continuity.

Regular check-ins prevent drift: Each month, review whether:

- Decisions are changing because of the data.
- Collection remains consistent.
- Data quality is high.
- Stakeholders still find value.

If any answer is "no," adjust.

Common System Failures

Understanding predictable failure modes helps you avoid them.

Feature creep: Starting simple but gradually adding complexity until the system becomes unwieldy. Resist the temptation to add new metrics simply because you can.

Single point of failure: Building processes that depend on one person's expertise or presence. Always have backup operators and clearly documented protocols.

Data hoarding: Collecting information "just in case" rather than for specific decisions. This wastes bandwidth for relevant collection and creates noise that hides important signals.

Technology dependence: Building systems that collapse when technology fails rather than reverting smoothly to simpler alternatives.

Stakeholder drift: Losing touch with whether users still find the approach valuable as their needs evolve.

PRACTITIONER PERSPECTIVE

Q: What is the most important lesson you have learned about creating structured routines or workflows ("systems") in sport science that remain effective and sustainable over time?

ANNA CRUSE, MS

"Systems take work, constant development, and require feedback from users. I think a common misconception is that once you have a system in place, it will continue working forever. In reality, creating effective systems requires change and adaptation.

Additionally, when implementing a high functioning, well-tested system in a new environment, remember that people are part of the system. A system that's well oiled in one environment might have a hitch in another. The people who interact with your system matter. Seek out feedback from them to make it as effective as possible."

▶ **ANNA CRUSE**
Director, Applied Health & Performance | University of Utah

📝 Your System Building Action Plan

Week 1: Choose Your Target

- Identify one decision you make regularly that affects athlete performance or safety.
- Apply the **Three-Question Test (Chapter 2)** to define information needs clearly.
- Document your current decision-making process and information sources.

Week 2: Design Minimum Viable System

- Choose the simplest data collection method that could improve your decision.
- Create specific action protocols for different scenarios.
- Identify who will collect data and when it will be reviewed.

Week 3: Test and Adjust

- Run your system for one week, tracking both data and decision-making changes.
- Gather feedback from all stakeholders involved.
- Document what worked well and what created friction.

Week 4: Stabilize and Document

- Make one key improvement based on Week 3 learning.
- Write down your protocols and backup plans.
- Establish a regular review schedule for ongoing maintenance.

Month 2: Gradual Expansion

- Only after your core system runs smoothly for four weeks should you consider additions.
- Add one element at a time, ensuring each stabilizes before adding more.
- Continue regular stakeholder feedback and system audits.

Integration with Context

Effective approaches reflect the context awareness introduced in Chapter 2.

Resource-constrained environments: Enhance existing processes rather than creating new ones. Use technology already available and leverage established relationships and routines.

Well-resourced environments: Take advantage of capabilities while maintaining focus on specific decisions. More resources allow comprehensive approaches but shouldn't replace simplicity where it's more effective.

Team environments: Design systems that work across athletes with varying needs. Create clear protocols for handling individual variation within team frameworks.

The most effective systems deliver the right information to the right people at the right time. What matters is action, not sophistication. A system only matters when its output drives action that improves performance. In the next chapter, we'll shift from structure to signal, and explore how to turn system outputs into communication that reliably drives decisions.

Effective systems start with clear purpose and deliver consistent, actionable insights.

 KEY TAKEAWAYS

BUILD SYSTEMS THAT ACTUALLY WORK

- Start with the decisions you need to make, not just the data you can collect.
- Keep systems simple, sustainable, and integrated into daily routines.
- Build trust through early wins, stakeholder buy-in, and regular review.

4

MAKE INFORMATION ACTIONABLE

"If you want people to make the right decisions with data, you have to get in their head in a way they understand."

MIRO KAZAKOFF

BIG ROCK #3

Make Information Actionable

A SPORT SCIENTIST presented a 30-page report filled with colorful graphs and complex statistics to a college football coaching staff. The presentation lasted 45 minutes and covered everything from weight room performance to high-speed running trends. When it ended, the head coach flipped through the document and asked a simple question: "So what should we do at practice today?"

Silence.

All that data and all those analyses, yet no clear direction. The sport scientist had transformed numbers into charts but missed the critical step of turning information into practical decision opportunities.

In contrast, another program summarized the same concepts in a single slide. Instead of dozens of charts, the dashboard displayed clear training guidance: session duration, live-contact minutes, and daily readiness status, along with short notes for discussion. Coaches could review it in seconds, talk it through with the performance staff, and make adjustments before practice began.

This example captures the essence of our third Big Rock: **Make Information Actionable**. Collecting data and producing beautiful visuals isn't enough. The real value of sport science comes from offering information that guides action, shapes meaningful conversations, and supports better-informed decisions.

The Communication Challenge

Across hundreds of sport science programs, the same pattern repeats: the gap between having information and acting on it. That's where most systems fail. Teams invest enormous effort collecting and analyzing data but struggle to turn insights into clear, applied guidance.

Two professional soccer teams used identical monitoring systems. The first delivered long weekly reports full of charts and commentary. They looked impressive, but coaches lacked the time to turn them into daily plans. The reports were reviewed once, then forgotten.

The second team used the same data but communicated it differently. Each morning, coaches received a one-page summary with color-coded player preparedness scores and short, plain-language recommendations. The performance staff joined the coaches in brief discussions before practice to interpret results and adjust the plan, together. The information became a shared language, not a technical report. Same data. Same analysis. Completely different impact. The difference was communication that matched the environment, the people, and how decisions were made. Making information actionable isn't only about simplifying the science; it's about connecting the science to action.

THE ACTIONABILITY TEST

This test verifies that your insights are ready to drive behavior instead of simply increasing awareness. Before presenting information to stakeholders, you should be able to answer four questions:

1. What specific action should result from this information?
2. Who has the authority to take this action?
3. When must they act for it to be effective?
4. What negative consequence occurs if no action is taken?

If you can't answer all four clearly, the information isn't ready to be presented and shared.

Visual Communication That Drives Action

Effective visualization turns complex data into immediate understanding when it's designed with purpose. The aim isn't to create impressive charts or fancy dashboards; it's to make better decisions, faster.

A professional ice hockey team struggled with morning readiness assessments until they replaced complex dashboards with a simple word cloud built from daily athlete comments. When many players responded with words like "tired," "sore," or "stressed," those words appeared larger, revealing patterns the staff could address. Before players arrived, the coaches could take a glance at the word cloud and immediately understand the group's overall mood. This helped them set the right tone in conversations as players entered the training environment and gave them an opportunity to adjust on-ice workloads so the work matched how the team felt. The visualization served a specific purpose: it turned abstract wellbeing responses into a clear read on team mood that coaches could use right away to choose better actions.

The system worked because it was simple and action-oriented. Instead of forcing coaches to scroll through spreadsheets, the visualization highlighted collective patterns and directed them to the actions that mattered. Once the decision is defined, present information in a way that drives purposeful action.

THE GLANCE TEST

Effective visualizations should pass the three-second rule. If someone can't understand the main message and required action within three seconds, simplify the visualization **(Figure 12)**. The faster people understand what the data means, the faster they can act on it. That's the true measure of an effective visualization. It enables the audience to act on the right information quickly and confidently.

But speed isn't enough. The best visuals require very little mental effort to interpret. They make people want to look, not avoid looking. When information feels intuitive and accessible, coaches and athletes engage with it more consistently. That's what makes visualization truly effective: it lowers the barrier to understanding and drives confident, consistent action.

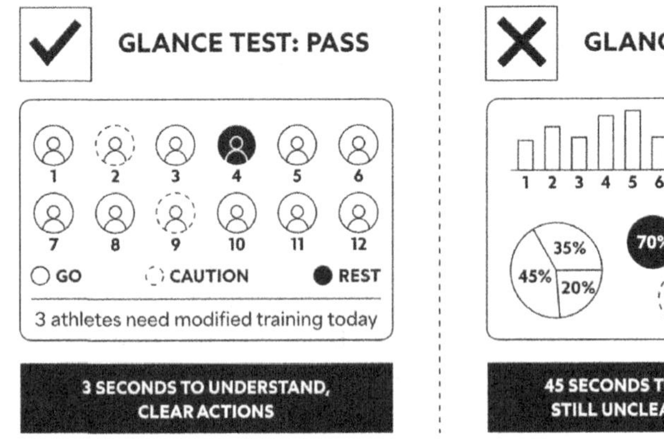

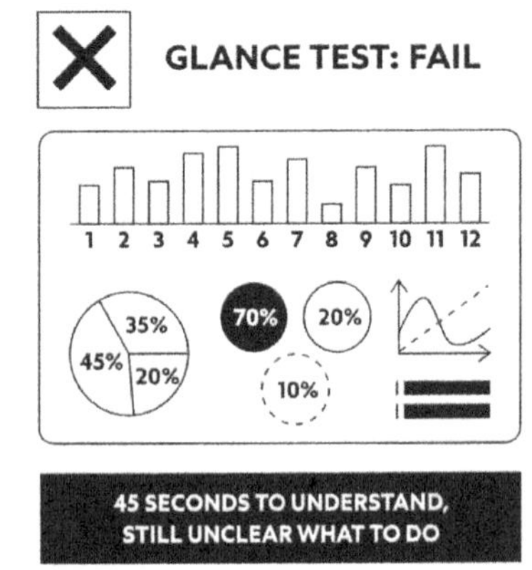

Figure 12. *The Glance Test: Clear visualization design enables three-second understanding and immediate action, while cluttered design creates confusion and delays decisions.*

Essential Principles for Action-Oriented Visualization

Start with the decision: Before creating any visual, define what decision it should inform and what potential actions could result. Then design backward from that endpoint. A visualization that doesn't contribute to a decision is decoration, not communication.

Put important information where people look first: People naturally read in a consistent direction, generally top to bottom and left to right (or right to left, depending on the writing system). Structure content so that the most important insights appear where the eyes go first. Lead with the essential message or visuals, then provide supporting context below or to the side. When information is organized in this natural reading order, users can scan quickly, understand effortlessly, and act with confidence.

Make the next step obvious: Don't just show status; clearly indicate what should happen next. Color-coded systems work because they naturally suggest actions: green for go, yellow for caution, red for stop. (Note: Always pair color with position, icons, or text to ensure accessibility.) Good visualization design reduces hesitation by connecting insight to behavior.

Always explain why numbers matter: A raw change is meaningless without context. Saying "sprint time increased by 0.20 seconds" tells you nothing. Saying "sprint time increased by 0.20 seconds, which is concerning because we are in competition season" signals a red flag. Saying "sprint time increased by 0.20 seconds, which is expected during the strength training phase" means there is no concern. The same number can have very different meanings depending on timing and context. Whether it's shown in text or through visuals, the same rule applies.

A college gymnastics team discovered this when they replaced detailed performance charts with simple status cards for each athlete. Each card showed the current preparedness level, the trend direction (improving, stable, or declining), and the specific training recommendations. Coaches reported making faster, more confident decisions because information clearly pointed toward appropriate actions.

Visual Design That Drives Action

The same principles that make data actionable also apply to design. Yet even with the right mindset, many practitioners struggle with the practical side of visual communication.

Imagine trying to navigate a city with a map that has no street names, no landmarks, and everything printed in tiny, upside-down text. Even if the map is technically accurate, you would feel confused and overwhelmed, and probably end up getting lost. Poor data visuals create the same problem. They slow you down and add confusion when you need clarity most. Well-designed visuals act like clean, readable maps. They help people find key information quickly, understand what it means, and decide what to do next. Clear design transforms information from something that must be interpreted into something that guides action.

Four design principles make that possible. They transform static data displays into fast, effective decision-making tools that help practitioners act with confidence.

1. **Reduce clutter**: Every extra element, such as unnecessary borders, background shading, or excessive labels, adds visual noise that distracts from your message. Remove anything that doesn't directly support decision-making.
2. **Improve readability**: Use large, legible fonts, intuitive color schemes, and appropriate chart types. This reduces cognitive load and speeds understanding for busy practitioners. "Cool" fonts rarely help communication; prioritize clarity over style.
3. **Provide context**: Raw numbers lack meaning without reference points. Always include comparisons to historical information, group norms, or expected ranges so users can immediately tell whether a value is good, bad, or concerning.
4. **Order information flow**: Structure layouts so the most important insights appear first and are visually prominent. This allows coaches to capture key takeaways at a glance and explore details only when needed.

These four principles work together to create visualizations that drive action, not confusion **(Figure 13)**. Other factors, such as chart type, spacing, axis integrity, and accessibility, also matter. But the goal is always the same: clear, usable information that enables faster, more informed decisions.

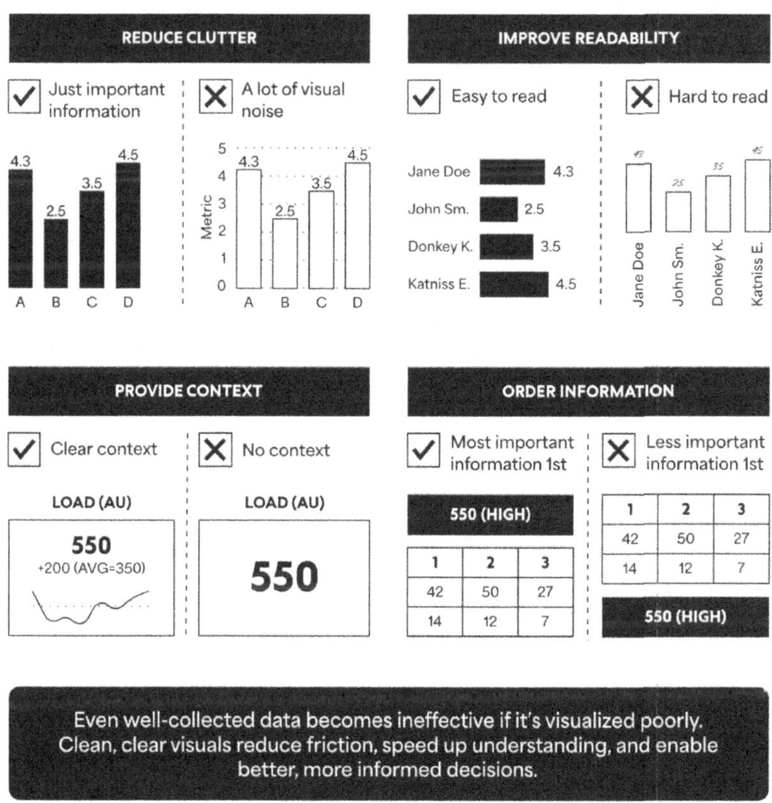

Figure 13. *Four essential design principles for actionable data visualization: reduce clutter, improve readability, provide context, and order information flow.*

PRACTITIONER PERSPECTIVE

Q: What core principle or approach ensures your data visualizations clearly translate complex data into actionable insights for coaches or athletes?

JOHANN WINDT, PhD

"***Start with the end in mind, and then build to that end****. In applied sport, this is vital. Data visualization in sport science is meant for exactly this purpose: informing decisions of varying stakeholders such as executives, coaches, and athletes. My core principle for ensuring that my visualizations are a means to this end is to start with the end in mind, and then build the data visualization in a way that gets to that end. Let me elaborate.*

Start with the end in mind*. As I think about a given data visualization, who is the audience/decision maker that's going to be looking at it? What is the decision(s) that they're going to have to make that this visualization may help them to be more informed? How frequently will they need to look at the visualization? Where and how are they going to be consuming this visualization (e.g., on their phone, computer, etc.)? Instead of imagining just how the chart or dashboard may look, I try to think about the broader context in which the visualization is going to be delivered and imagine the executive, coach, or athlete actually making the necessary decision.*

Build to that end*. The best data visualization in the world is rendered basically useless if it doesn't empower the decision maker who it has been designed for. Therefore, having thought through all the principles above, I do all that I can to maximize the likelihood that my visualization can effectively inform decision making. The ways that I've found success in most instances include:*

- *Meet and discuss. The stories I have of visualizations that have informed decisions and had the greatest impact in the environments I have worked in are not of dashboards – but they're visuals that myself or my team presented directly to decision makers either privately or in a meeting. This is perhaps the most important learning to drive impact: build them as visualizations so that they can communicate effectively without anyone explaining them but always try to present and explain them directly as well. This human presentation allows for consideration, discussion, debate, clarification, and further follow-up. It also guarantees that the decision maker looks at the visualization.*

- *Actively notify/email. Although you can't have a meeting every time a visualization is released, I don't think it's wise to simply update or add dashboards/visualizations and assume that people are going to self-discover and actively use those dashboards. Even without a meeting, it's important to take an active approach to data visualization delivery to increase the likelihood that people will use the information. Email remains incredibly valuable and is often the best delivery strategy. I absolutely love interactive visualizations, smart tooltips, click-through charts, etc., but I've consistently found the many people are more likely to still open their email and look at a static chart than go to a dashboard to find the information.*

- *Minimize clicks and time to understanding. People working in sport are busy, and many won't voluntarily sift through tables to find insights. Maximize accessibility and make it as easy as possible to access, and then understand your visualizations. If online, embed it where people already go, send it directly to the decision maker. Make visuals clear with informative titles and accurate axes. Finally, don't be afraid to call out the point especially if presenting the visual in a meeting, don't bury the lead. If a visual is supposed to be supporting a specific decision recommendation, state the recommendation clearly and show the figure as a supporting point for discussion* ***(Figure 14)****.*"

► **JOHANN WINDT**

Founder | Cascaid Health

DOMINIC SAMANGY, MS

"Success in conveying information at the highest levels of sport hinges on keeping communication simple, consistent, and reliable. Whether it's a coach explaining a defensive scheme, an athlete sharing on-court cues, or medical staff outlining a rehab plan, the most effective messages are delivered quickly and clearly. As a data analyst, I apply the same principles. I prioritize simplicity through tables, bar charts, and time series line graphs rather than complex visualizations. I ensure consistency through familiar color scales and reference points like percentiles or team ranks. Finally, when needed, I establish reliability by clearly explaining how data is collected, why it matters, and how it can inform action."

► **DOMINIC SAMANGY**
Basketball Analytics Coordinator | New Orleans Pelicans

DANIEL YU, MS

"My core principle is to design visualizations around the question being asked. This ensures the data directly supports a decision. Keeping visuals simple and focused helps the audience quickly understand what matters. Even the title can be framed as the answer to the question.

For example, if a coach asks how to optimize an athlete's training, I might present a line graph of the athlete's heart rate variability (HRV) over the past month. I would remove unnecessary elements like x-axis labels since dates are obvious and that makes the visual more focused. To make the data meaningful, I would add thresholds marking HRV levels outside of their normal range that may indicate overtraining or undertraining risk and use color to highlight when the athlete is outside those ranges. This way, the coach can clearly see when adjustments are needed and make data-informed decisions."

► **DANIEL YU**
Applied Sport Scientist & Assistant Strength and Conditioning Coach | Orlando Magic

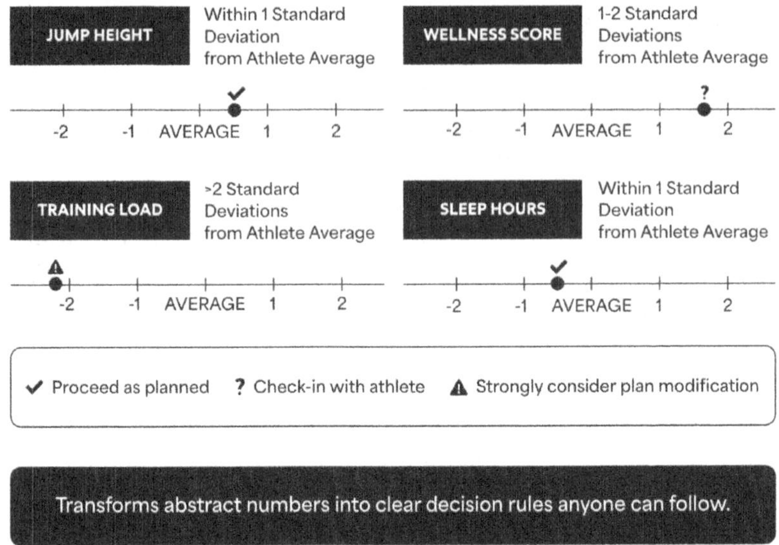

Figure 14. *Decision-making framework: Converting standardized data into clear action rules that enable consistent, confident choices without requiring complex interpretation.*

Designing for Your Audience

Even the clearest insight loses its value if it is delivered the wrong way. Making information actionable means matching the message to the people who need it. Different stakeholders seek different things, so your role is to speak their language and connect data to what matters in their world.

For Coaches:

Focus on performance implications and practical recommendations. Connect data to what they already observe, use their terminology rather than technical jargon, and provide options rather than directives when possible.

Example: "Three midfielders are showing patterns we typically see before performance drops in games. Consider rotating them more frequently in today's scrimmage."

For Athletes:

Explain how data relates to how they feel and perform. Use visual comparisons to their own previous data, connect recommendations to their personal goals, and keep explanations concise and actionable.

Example: "Your GPS data suggests you're not completing enough high-intensity actions to perform optimally during competition. Focus on resting enough in between bouts during today's skill work to help produce higher-intensity efforts."

For Medical Staff:

Provide more technical detail about measurement methods, focus on risk factors and early warning indicators, and connect to existing medical protocols.

Example: "Current fatigue markers and reduced calf-strength measurements indicate elevated soft-tissue injury risk during practice this week. Monitor for early signs of hamstring or calf tightness, particularly in the three players flagged in this morning's report."

These are not scripts to follow, but examples of how to frame information in ways that resonate with different audiences. A tailored approach ensures insights drive behavior rather than being ignored or misunderstood. Each stakeholder receives the information required to take effective action within their role and responsibilities.

The Multiple Perspectives Principle

There is an old parable about blind men encountering an elephant. Each touches a different part: the trunk, the leg, the side, the tail. Each believes they're touching something completely different from one another. Only by sharing their perspectives do they realize the truth: they're all touching the same elephant.

Sport science works the same way. Each stakeholder holds a distinct but incomplete view.

- **The athlete** knows how they feel, what hurts, and what feels different from normal.

- **The coach** observes technical changes, motivational shifts, and how the athlete fits into team strategy and rhythm.
- **The medical and training staff** understand injury history, physical limitations, and recovery capacity.
- **The sport scientist** connects information across domains, analyzing trends, interpreting data, and identifying patterns that support better decisions.

No single perspective tells the full story. An American football player may show normal physiological markers while feeling drained from academic stress. A basketball player's jump performance may decline not from fatigue but from a minor ankle issue that has not been reported. Data should never stand alone. It gains meaning only when combined with the shared observations, experiences, and expertise of the people who know the athletes best.

The best decisions in sport science rarely come from one source of truth. They emerge from conversation between coaches, athletes, medical staff, and sport scientists, each contributing their perspective to build a clearer picture and make better choices for the athlete.

MENTAL MODEL MOMENT

CIRCLE OF COMPETENCE

Key Principle: Know what you understand well, and more importantly, what you don't. Most errors come from overconfidence in areas that we don't actually understand.

When reviewing data, instead of thinking, "This athlete needs rest," consider, "What other perspectives have been shared? The data may suggest fatigue, but we should also weigh what the coach has observed and how the athlete feels before deciding."

This is the essence of staying within your circle of competence. Know where your expertise begins and where it ends, and rely on others to complete the picture **(Figure 15)**.

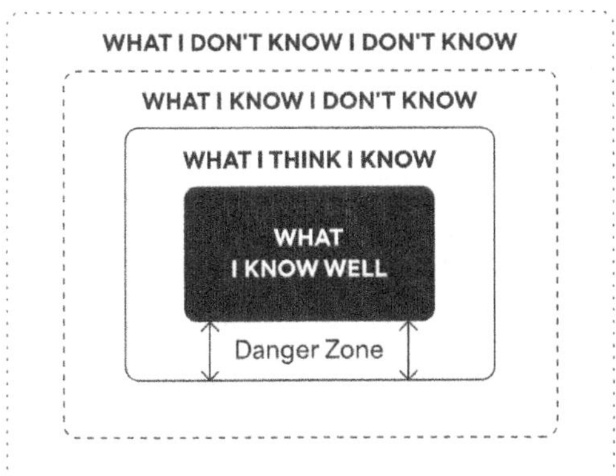

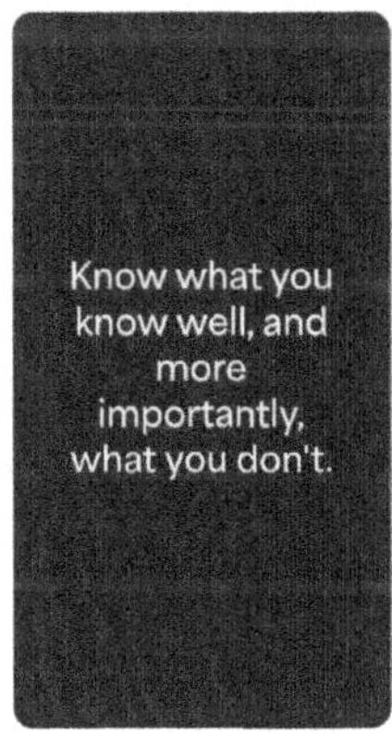

Figure 15. *Circle of competence: Understanding the boundaries of your expertise prevents overconfidence and enables better collaboration by leveraging others' specialized knowledge.*

Building Trust Through Clear Communication

Without trust, nothing else matters. Trust grows when people understand your reasoning, see your process is transparent, and recognize your recommendations align with shared goals.

A cricket team strengthened confidence in their bowling workload system by beginning with metrics coaches already valued. They validated coaches' intuitions about fatigue, then introduced new insights only after connecting each to visible performance changes. Experienced coaches often have valuable intuitions through years of observation. By demonstrating how data supports those instincts, you can establish credibility that fosters acceptance of new ideas. Even when they challenge long-held beliefs.

Transparency means being clear about limitations. When an American football team's monitoring system suggested a player needed rest, the sport scientist explained both reasoning and uncertainty: "His back squat barbell velocity is down 5-10 percent from baseline for three straight lifting sessions. This may indicate accumulated fatigue,which can affect route-running performance. However, it could also reflect measurement variation or other factors not captured in our system."

This kind of honesty builds trust. It shows you understand both the power and the limits of the data.

Creating Visual Stories

Charts and dashboards rarely change behavior on their own. People act when they understand the story behind the numbers. The most actionable information follows a simple narrative structure that links three elements: what is happening, why it matters, and what should be done next. Without that structure, even accurate data becomes noise.

Set the Context

Every visualization should answer: Why does this matter? What are we trying to understand?

Example: A rugby team's injury prevention presentation started with the question: "How can we keep our key players healthy during the final month of the season?"

Present the Key Finding

Focus on the single most important insight rather than trying to communicate everything at once.

Example: The analysis showed that players who are experiencing high training loads and poor sleep are 3.5 times more likely to sustain injuries the following week.

Explain the Implications

Connect the finding to outcomes that matter to your audience.

Example: "This pattern suggests we can significantly reduce injury risk by modifying training load and improving sleep quality."

Recommend Specific Actions

End with direct, practical guidance. Avoid vague phrases such as "monitor closely" or "consider adjustments." Make it clear what should happen next.

Example: "Implement daily sleep check-ins and adjust training intensity for any player showing both high load and poor sleep."

This simple narrative transforms raw data into a story that moves people from understanding to action.

Practical Communication Frameworks

When time is short, structure helps. Simple formats show what matters and what to do next. Here are a few examples of how to turn "interesting numbers" into clear decisions.

The Traffic Light Report

Organize information into three categories:

- **Color 1** (for example, blue): Continue as planned.
- **Color 2** (for example, orange): Monitor closely.
- **Color 3** (for example, red): Immediate attention required.

This framework works for any information type and immediately communicates priority levels.

THE "SO WHAT?" TEST

Before communicating an insight, make sure it connects to a clear decision. Ask yourself three simple questions:

- So, what does this mean?
- So, what should we do about it?
- So, what happens if we do nothing?

The Status Dashboard

Present current information in a format that drives immediate action. One baseball team created individual pitcher cards displaying pitch count, trend direction, and specific recommendations. Coaches could review the entire pitching staff within seconds and decide who needed conversations about potential workload adjustments.

The Context Timeline

Displaying data over time helps reveal trends and causes. Pair current information with the context that shaped it. A basketball coach might notice a drop in high-intensity actions, then realize it coincides with recent travel demands. Or, perhaps the pattern appears against slower-paced opponents. Seeing performance change in context prevents overreaction. It helps staff respond with understanding rather than panic.

Making Data Conversations, Not Presentations

The best communication happens through conversation, not lecture. Sport science isn't about handing people conclusions. Rather, it's about creating discussions where data meets real-world experience.

A volleyball team improved their weekly reviews by replacing formal slide presentations with short, guided discussions. The sport scientist shared two or three key observations, then asked coaches and athletes what they thought might explain the patterns and what adjustments made sense.

This back-and-forth uncovered insights that charts alone couldn't reveal and built stronger ownership of the decisions that followed. The purpose of these conversations isn't to have every answer, but to ask the questions that help people connect information to what they see, feel, and know.

📝 Your Actionable Information Action Plan

Knowing what makes information actionable is one thing. Building the habit is another. This four-week plan helps you put the principles into practice. Take it one step at a time, sharpen your approach, and learn what works best in your environment and with your stakeholders.

Week 1: Audit Current Communication

- Review your last three reports or data presentations.
- Apply the **Actionability Test** to each.
- Identify which insights led to decisions and which were ignored.
- Record any feedback from coaches, athletes, or staff about clarity and usefulness.

Week 2: Design for Decisions

- Choose one recurring decision that could benefit from clearer information.
- Apply the **Glance Test**: can people understand the key message within three seconds?
- Create a simple visual using a Traffic Light or Status Dashboard format.
- Test it with stakeholders and gather honest feedback.

Week 3: Tailor to Audiences

- Select two or three different stakeholder groups who receive the same information.
- Present one key insight in distinct versions for each group.
- Focus on what each group needs to know to take effective action.

- Note which version sparks the strongest understanding and engagement within each group.

Week 4: Practice Storytelling

- Choose one complex dataset and apply the three-step story structure: what's happening, why it matters, and what should be done next (always considering context).
- Share it both in conversation and as a visual story.
- Gather feedback on which version creates faster understanding and better decisions.
- Record what you learn to strengthen future communication.

Common Communication Failures

Information overload: Presenting everything you know instead of what people need to act. More information rarely leads to better decisions.

Technical language: Using terms that confuse instead of clarify. If someone needs a translator, the message has failed.

Analysis without synthesis: Showing patterns without explaining what they mean or what to do next.

One-size-fits-all reporting: Using the same format for coaches, athletes, and staff, even though each interprets data differently and prefers distinct ways of communicating.

Overstating certainty: Presenting uncertainty as fact, which erodes trust when reality proves otherwise.

Action ambiguity: Ending without clear next steps, leaving people unsure what to do.

Connecting with Previous Big Rocks

Actionable information builds on both context and systems:

Context alignment: Match information complexity to the audience's capacity to process and act on that information. A traffic-light summary of training load data may work best for busy coaches, while deeper analysis may be better suited for experienced practitioners.

System reliability: Clear visuals mean little if the underlying data are inconsistent or incomplete. Reliable systems produce reliable insights through consistent collection, clear processes, and regular review. When systems are stable, insights become trustworthy and decisions become repeatable.

Decision focus: Every context assessment and system design should center on specific decisions. When that foundation is in place, actionability follows naturally.

The best programs do more than collect and analyze data. They turn insights into clear, timely guidance that helps people make better decisions day after day. That bridge between analysis and action often determines whether sport science creates value or becomes another expensive distraction. From making information actionable, we move to our next challenge: working with uncertainty. Even the cleanest visualizations and clearest communication can't eliminate a fundamental reality. Every measurement has limits, and every decision involves judgment under imperfect information.

Effective sport science turns information into guidance that drives confident, informed action.

 KEY TAKEAWAYS

MAKE INFORMATION ACTIONABLE

- Design communication to directly inform clear, timely decisions.
- Use simple, targeted visuals that pass the "glance test."
- Tailor delivery to your audience to ensure understanding and action.

5

EMBRACE UNCERTAINTY

"We are prone to overestimate how much we understand about the world and to underestimate the role of chance."

DANIEL KAHNEMAN

Embrace Uncertainty

A TRACK COACH ONCE SHOWED us two nearly identical datasets from his sprinters' training logs. Same athletes. Same exercises. Same measurement setup. Yet one stretch of training led to season-best performances, and the other preceded a run of injuries and disappointing results.

"Can you tell which is which?" the coach asked.

We couldn't. The numbers looked almost the same. Training loads were normal, readiness scores were steady, and performance metrics followed expected patterns. Only when the track coach explained the context did the difference appear: the successful period happened in ideal weather with consistent schedules, while the disappointing period fell during exam week with little sleep and high stress.

That moment captures our fourth Big Rock: **Embrace Uncertainty.** No matter how advanced our tools or detailed our data, we are always working with incomplete information. The athlete's full reality stretches far beyond what any system can record.

The best sport scientists don't fight uncertainty. They account for it in their decisions. They learn to find signals in the noise, to question evidence thoughtfully, and to act confidently even when information is imperfect.

The Reality of Measurement Uncertainty

Sport science always involves uncertainty. Every measurement carries error, every athlete responds differently, and many unseen factors lie behind the numbers we see.

MENTAL MODEL MOMENT

THE MAP IS NOT THE TERRITORY

Key Principle: Any data, model, or plan is a simplification of reality. Mistakes happen when we assume our representations are reality itself.

Consider what we are really measuring when we assess readiness. Heart-rate variability might reflect recovery, but it can also change with caffeine intake and the time of day. Wellness questionnaires capture how athletes feel, but responses can be shaped by mood, expectations, and the desire to give socially acceptable answers. Jump tests estimate power, but technique, motivation, footwear, and floor surface all influence the outcome.

None of these metrics are wrong. They're simply incomplete views of complex, ever-changing systems. A force plate result that suggests an athlete is ready doesn't guarantee they truly are. Always cross-check the data with context, observation, and athlete feedback. Uncertainty can't be erased. Effective sport science doesn't eliminate uncertainty; it works with it. Measurements are maps, not the territory itself **(Figure 16)**.

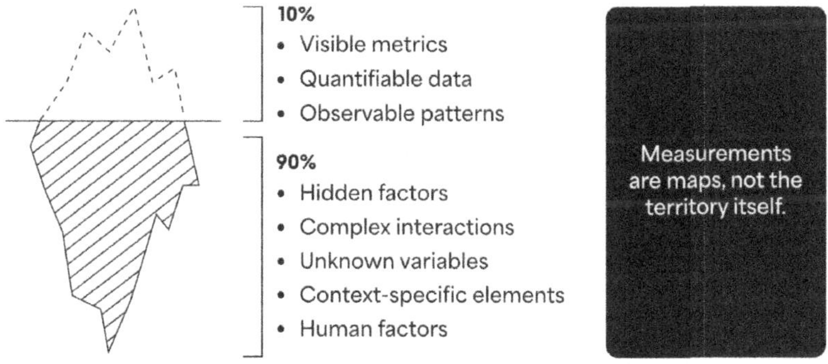

Figure 16. *The map is not the territory: Measurements capture only a small portion of complex athletic performance, with most influencing factors remaining hidden or unmeasurable.*

Understanding Measurement Quality

Error is inevitable, and it comes in all shapes and sizes. What separates good measurement from bad is understanding error and its sources well enough to make sound decisions.

Let's use a bathroom scale to understand key qualities of measurement. Validity (accuracy) means the scale shows your true weight. Reliability (precision or consistency) means it gives the same number every time you step on. Sensitivity (responsiveness) means it detects even small, real changes. Understanding these qualities helps you trust what your data are really saying.

Types of Measurement Error

Systematic error: Produces consistent bias in one direction, such as a scale that always reads five pounds heavy. Once identified, it can often be corrected through calibration.

Random error: Creates unpredictable variation even when measuring the same thing repeatedly. It often comes from small differences in setup, environmental changes, or device limitations.

Human error: Introduces variability through inconsistent protocols or data entry mistakes. Clear and standardized procedures help reduce it.

Oversight error: Occurs when data collection seems correct, but unseen contextual factors distort the results. For example, an athlete wearing reversible shorts might flip them inside out. This reverses the orientation of a waistband-mounted GPS unit, so accelerations register as decelerations and vice versa. In another case, a vibrating heat pack worn during training could create constant micro-movements that artificially inflate training load metrics. Without recognizing these hidden influences, staff may interpret clean-looking data as accurate and make misinformed decisions.

This is why "data-driven decisions" are ill-advised. Data alone shouldn't drive anything. Good decisions come from people who understand how the data were collected, recognize potential sources of error, and interpret results within the right context.

A collegiate volleyball program learned how measurement error can distort interpretation and decision quality when their daily jump testing showed wild fluctuations. Some athletes appeared to gain and lose 15 percent of their jump height from one day to the next. The issue wasn't the athletes, but the process. Testing protocols varied between staff members, the jump mat produced different readings on different floor surfaces, and testing times shifted across days. Once the staff standardized their procedures, measurement error dropped significantly, allowing them to better distinguish true change from noise.

Perfect data don't exist. The goal is to understand your data's limitations well enough to make good decisions despite them.

Establishing Reliability Thresholds

Before using any new assessment, perform at least three consecutive tests on the same athlete under identical conditions. Calculate both the mean value (average) and the typical error (the standard deviation or coefficient of variation across trials). This simple process reveals your system's reliability and helps establish thresholds for identifying "real" change.

Always compare new results to your typical measurement error before interpreting them. If the observed change falls within your system's normal variation, it may simply reflect noise. For example, if your testing method typically varies by three percent, then a two-percent difference is likely not meaningful. Only treat changes that exceed your typical error as potentially real.

Distinguishing Signal from Noise

When working with uncertain data, the goal is to determine when a change truly matters. Resist the urge to react to normal day-to-day variation; instead, look for consistent shifts or patterns that move beyond expected ranges **(Figure 17)**.

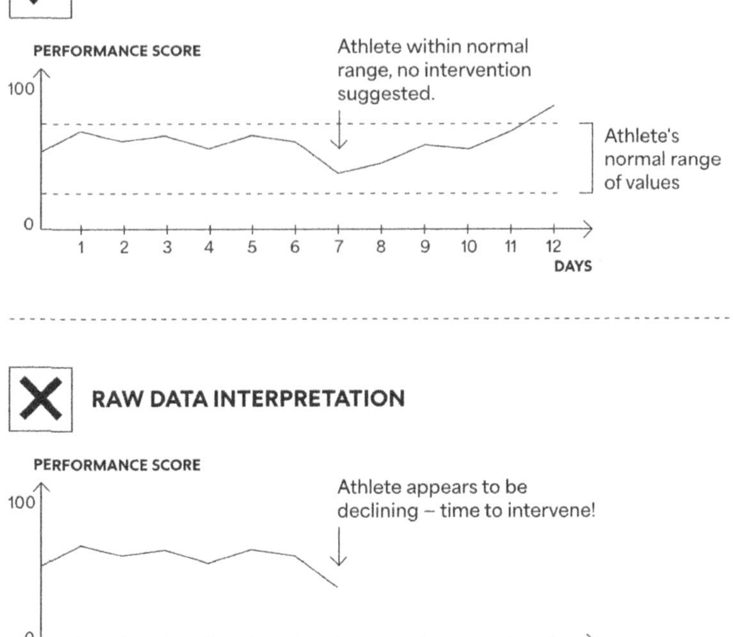

Figure 17. *Signal vs. noise analysis: Effective data interpretation identifies meaningful patterns that warrant intervention rather than reacting to normal daily variation.*

When Statistics Meet Practice

When research reports "statistically significant ($p < 0.05$)" results, it simply means the observed difference was unlikely to occur by random chance. It doesn't mean the effect was large, important, or relevant to your athletes.

Think of statistical significance like a smoke detector: it can tell you something unusual is happening, but not whether it's burnt toast or a house fire. What matters most is **practical significance**: how big the effect is and whether it actually impacts performance. Ask, *Is this improvement big enough to matter in my setting?* A one-percent improvement in a 100-meter sprint could be the difference between silver and gold. That same one percent in a marathon might barely move the standings.

Defining Meaningful Change

Once reliability and variability are known, the next step is defining when a change is real and relevant. Develop clear, context-specific guidelines to interpret results:

Small but meaningful change: The smallest improvement that athletes or coaches can perceive as helpful, even if it isn't statistically significant. This often corresponds to roughly one to two times the typical error of measurement.

Performance-relevant change: A shift large enough to meaningfully affect competition outcomes or training decisions in your specific sport or environment.

Risk-related change: A consistent pattern that aligns with elevated risk for fatigue, injury, or other negative outcomes within your context.

For example, if jump height testing typically varies by about three percent, you might treat any change smaller than three percent as noise, a three-to-six-percent shift as small but potentially meaningful, and anything greater than six percent as clearly actionable. Statistical thresholds help filter random noise, while performance-based thresholds determine when to intervene.

PRACTITIONER PERSPECTIVE

Q: What are two to three foundational statistical or research principles you believe every practitioner should clearly understand?

PATRICK WARD, PhD

STRENGTH COACHES, PHYSICAL THERAPISTS, AND TRAINERS:

"For strength coaches, physical therapists, and athletic trainers, I think there is a lot of value in knowing a few types of summary statistics, what they mean, how they differ with respect to the bits of information they can provide, and how they can be used. Things like mean, standard deviation, standard error, median, median absolute deviation, and interquartile range can be incredibly valuable for the applied practitioner in understanding base rates and conducting basic analysis and subgroup analysis to explore some fundamental numbers behind the data they collect. Additionally, the basics of measurement principles (validity, reliability, sensitivity, interpretability) should be something that applied practitioners have a good understanding of. They don't need to know how to necessarily conduct all the analysis or set up research methods to explore such concepts, but they should be aware of how measurement is conducted and the data behind them in order to be more discerning and critical of the data they collect and how they can collect data in a more principled way."

APPLIED ANALYSIS PRACTITIONERS:

"For applied analysis practitioners, the same understanding of measurement theory as the applied practitioner is relevant along with the ability to conduct measurement research, analyze the data specific to different questions, and have a strong fundamental knowledge of research methods. Scientific theory is important for this group of practitioners. Recent graduates are often very adept at writing code, tuning models, and working with data. However, they often lack the ability to clearly formulate a research question, understand different assumptions behind their research methods, or know how to test and validate models. These

are skills that need to be cultivated to help them take the next steps as an applied analyst. Finally, understanding things like causal analysis and basic axioms of probability theory are critical for being able to navigate the messy environment of applied data."

▶ **PATRICK WARD**
Research & Development | Seattle Seahawks

ERNIE RIMER, PhD

"At the most fundamental level, every practitioner would benefit from understanding some of the most basic tenets of statistics: normality, standard deviation, regression, p-value, confidence interval, effect size, etc. Many of the more sophisticated statistical techniques depend on those foundations, which is why they're good to know."

▶ **ERNIE RIMER**
Director of Sport Science | University of Louisville

JENNY STRICKLER, PhD

"Foundational research principles every practitioner should understand include data quality and contextual analysis. First, fundamental concepts like validity and reliability are essential—especially in an industry saturated with technology and AI-driven tools. No matter how robust your statistical analyses are, meaningful insights depend on high-quality, trustworthy data. Second, it's critical to appropriately contextualize data, including intentional collection of relevant metadata and thoughtful subgrouping to avoid downstream masking or overstating of associations."

► **JENNY STRICKLER**
Director of Performance Science | Oklahoma City Thunder

MENTAL MODEL MOMENT

PROBABILISTIC THINKING

Key Principle: Think in probabilities, not certainties. Good decisions can still lead to bad outcomes, and vice versa.

Probabilistic Thinking

Probabilistic thinking means weighing how likely something is to be true rather than treating it as certain. Instead of asking, "Is this athlete ready?", ask, "How likely is this athlete to be ready?"

This mindset helps practitioners interpret imperfect data without overreacting to single results. It encourages decisions that balance evidence, uncertainty, and consequence rather than chasing false precision. Even strong data and validated systems only tell part of the story. Every conclusion is a likelihood, not a fact. Sport science involves thinking in ranges and confidence levels rather than absolutes.

A college basketball program applied probabilistic thinking when their monitoring system suggested a player was recovering well from injury. The objective data looked positive, but the player reported feeling "off." Instead of treating either source as definitive, the staff considered both as probabilities: a 80 percent chance of successful return based on objective markers and a 30 percent chance of underlying issues based on subjective feedback. Their plan reflected both realities, advancing carefully with continued monitoring. The approach reduced uncertainty and improved confidence in the return process.

Probabilistic thinking builds on everything discussed in this chapter, including measurement error, reliability, and meaningful change. By understanding variation and context, you can assign confidence to your conclusions instead of mistaking them for facts.

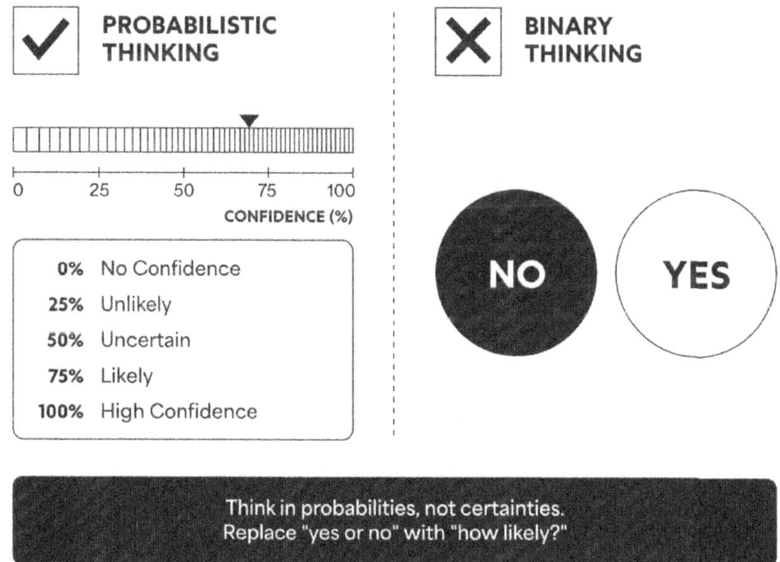

Figure 18. *Probabilistic thinking: Using confidence levels and likelihood assessments enables more nuanced decision-making than simple yes/no choices.*

Basic Research Evaluation Skills

Understanding research helps you judge claims and apply evidence effectively. You don't need to be an academic or a statistician, but you do need a reliable research "BS detector." Learning to spot weak claims, vague conclusions, and overstated findings helps you make better decisions in practice.

Fifteen-Minute Research Review

Research papers can be dense, but most of what matters can be uncovered in about fifteen minutes:

- **2 minutes:** Read the abstract to get the big picture.
- **5 minutes:** Review methods, including who was studied, how it was designed, what was measured, and how it was measured.
- **3 minutes:** Scan tables and figures to see what actually happened.
- **3 minutes:** Read the conclusions for how the authors interpret their findings.
- **2 minutes:** Note any listed limitations and critically evaluate other unnoted limitations.

The methods and results sections usually hold the truth. The introduction and discussion sections often reflect the authors' interpretations and opinions. Focus on how the study was conducted, what it assessed, and whether its findings truly apply to your environment.

Research Red Flags

Even well-written papers can hide major weaknesses. Certain signs should immediately raise skepticism:

- **Small sample size without acknowledgment of limitations**

  Example: A training supplement study claimed a 20 percent increase in strength, but it only included six college-aged men and didn't mention that limitation.

- **Multiple outcomes measured without proper statistical adjustment**

Example: A study found significant changes in high-speed distance and decelerations, but tested more than 50 GPS metrics, making false positives (e.g., finding a significant relationship) more likely than if only a few outcomes were analyzed.

- **Selective reporting of only favorable results**

  Example: A research group presented sprint data at a conference showing improvements after their new training program, but left out changes in other tests, like agility and jump height, that showed no change.

- **Overgeneralization beyond the studied population**

  Example: A soccer-specific warm-up routine is recommended for all sports, despite only being tested in 13-year-old female players.

- **Industry funding without transparent conflict of interest disclosure**

  Example: A wearable company funds a validation study and the paper claims "independent" evaluation, yet it fails to disclose that the company paid the researchers to conduct it.

- **No discussion of effect size or practical importance**

  Example: A recovery technique shows "statistically significant" improvement in fatigue scores, but the actual benefit was just 0.2 points on a 10-point scale.

These red flags don't automatically invalidate a study, but each one should make you more cautious. Ask whether the findings still make sense in your context and whether the evidence is strong enough to guide action.

Sample Size Reality

Small studies often miss real effects or overestimate them when they do appear. Be cautious with both null findings ("no significant effect") and dramatic claims ("massive 25 percent improvement") that come from limited samples. The smaller the study, the greater the uncertainty around its results.

An Australian Rules Football coach once avoided an expensive purchase by critically evaluating vendor research. The study showed impressive results, but it only included six participants over two weeks. When he looked at independent research with larger samples and longer timeframes, the effects were far smaller and likely not worth the investment.

Even when research is well designed, applying it in practice still involves uncertainty. Statistical results describe probabilities, not guarantees. The real skill lies in interpreting how confident you can be in those findings, and using that understanding to guide your next decision.

Making Decisions Under Uncertainty

Because decision-making in sport science rarely comes with perfect information, knowing how to act when confidence, clarity, and consequences vary is essential. Structured approaches such as the confidence–action framework help practitioners act decisively while acknowledging the limits of what they know **(Figure 19)**.

The Confidence–Action Framework

Match your response to your confidence level:

High Confidence + High Stakes + Clear Action: Act decisively and quickly. *A cyclist showing reduced heart rate recovery, poor sleep, decreased power, and increased exertion during championship week clearly needs rest.*

High Confidence + Low Stakes + Clear Action: Act decisively but with less urgency. *The same fatigue indicators during off-season training may suggest rest is ideal, but timing can be more flexible.*

High Confidence + High Stakes + Unclear Action: Proceed cautiously with expert input. *A track athlete might show perfect physiological markers but face family stress affecting motivation before major* *competition. Several intervention options exist, but choosing the right one is critical.*

High Confidence + Low Stakes + Unclear Action: Experiment thoughtfully. *The same scenario during the training phase allows testing different support approaches with lower risk.*

Low Confidence + High Stakes + Clear Action: Err on the side of caution. *If an athlete reports unusual pain before competition but intensive scans are normal, protect their health despite uncertainty.*

Low Confidence + Low Stakes + Clear Action: Take precautions. *The same pain scenario during routine training may only require monitoring and modified activity.*

Low Confidence + High Stakes + Unclear Action: Seek expert input with maximum safety measures. *Unclear symptoms before major competition require specialist consultation and protective protocols.*

Low Confidence + Low Stakes + Unclear Action: Focus on learning. *Minor issues during training provide an opportunity to gather better information and improve future decision-making.*

	HIGH CONFIDENCE		LOW CONFIDENCE	
	CLEAR ACTION	UNCLEAR ACTION	CLEAR ACTION	UNCLEAR ACTION
HIGH STAKES $$$	Act decisively and quickly	Act decisively with flexible timing	Proceed cautiously with expert consultation	Experiment thoughtfully
LOW STAKES $	Err strongly on side of caution	Take measured precautions	Seek expert input + maximum safety measures	Focus on gathering better information

Match your response to the confidence, clarity, and consequences of the situation.

Figure 19. *Confidence–action framework: A decision-making matrix that balances information certainty, stakes level, and action clarity to guide appropriate responses under uncertainty.*

Practical Decision Frameworks

In sport, important choices often come with little time and imperfect information. Making consistent decisions under pressure is difficult and mentally taxing. Frameworks provide structure in these moments. They help you slow down just enough to avoid reactive choices while still moving quickly enough to meet competitive demands. The following practical frameworks serve as mental shortcuts that make complex decisions more consistent, transparent, and defensible when pressure is high:

Convergent evidence approach: Require multiple, independent indicators before making major decisions. This reduces false alarms and prevents overreacting to a single data point.

Reversible decision strategy: Separate choices that can be easily changed (such as adjusting a single training session) from those with lasting consequences (such as changing an entire program).

Time-boxed trial method: Implement changes for a defined period with clear evaluation points rather than committing indefinitely to uncertain interventions.

Once a decision is made, the next challenge is communicating it. A framework strengthens your own reasoning, but transparency builds shared understanding and confidence. When others can follow how a decision was reached, they trust both the process and the people behind it.

Communicating Uncertainty Effectively

Few tasks in sport science are harder than explaining uncertainty while maintaining credibility. Practitioners must sound thoughtful, not hesitant. They need to come across as cautious because they care, not because they doubt themselves. How you frame information determines how others respond to it. Word choice matters.

Frame Uncertainty as Professional Caution

Instead of saying, "We are not sure what this means," try, "We are taking a cautious approach because athlete health and performance come first."

Provide context for confidence levels: "Based on three consistent indicators, we are highly confident this approach will help performance. We are monitoring two additional metrics to ensure we've not missed anything important."

Offer options with tradeoffs rather than single recommendations: "Option A provides higher performance potential with slightly increased injury risk. Option B offers a safer progression with more gradual gains."

Weather Forecast Language

A professional tennis program began describing training outcomes the way meteorologists describe weather. For a new serving drill, instead of saying it would help, they said: "There is an 80 percent chance this adjustment improves accuracy, a 15 percent chance of no change, and a 5 percent chance it throws off timing for a few sessions."

The shift changed how conversations unfolded. Framing expectations this way helped coaches and athletes interpret recommendations with realism and avoid both overconfidence and confusion.

Building Your Uncertainty Toolkit

Track Your Track Record

Document what you predicted and what actually happened. This habit builds awareness of your own decision patterns and helps separate genuine signals from noise. A simple log is enough:

- **Prediction or hypothesis**: What you expected to happen.
- **Confidence level**: How certain you felt (1–10 scale).
- **Outcome**: What occurred.
- **Lessons learned**: What this taught you about your judgment.

Calibrate Your Confidence

Compare your stated confidence to actual results. If you're correct about 90 percent of the time when you say you're "highly confident," your calibration is strong. If accuracy is closer to 60 percent, you're overconfident and can adjust accordingly.

Learn from Surprises

When reality doesn't match your expectations, analyze what you missed or misunderstood. These moments often reveal blind spots that lead to stronger decision-making in the future.

PRACTITIONER PERSPECTIVE

Q: What are two to three common statistical misunderstandings or misinterpretations you regularly encounter, and how do you address or avoid these in practice?

ERNIE RIMER, PhD

"Coaches and other practitioners commonly misinterpret what they see on a graph or chart unverified by statistical testing. It's quite easy to present a chart to convey a specific story that will influence decisions in favor of the illustrator's bias. Doing so without proper due diligence to verify what is seen is like wrapping garbage in glitter. By integrating appropriate underlying statistical diagnostics, sport scientists can add credibility to their reporting, ensuring proper interpretation by others."

► **ERNIE RIMER**
Director of Sport Science | University of Louisville

📝 Your Uncertainty Management Action Plan

Uncertainty isn't a flaw in sport science; it's a constant. Metrics fluctuate, research evolves, and human performance resists perfect prediction. Rather than treating uncertainty as the enemy, view it as part of reality. When interpreted carefully, uncertainty can sharpen decisions instead of clouding them. This four-week plan offers a structured process to test your measures, communicate probabilities, evaluate evidence, and apply decision frameworks so uncertainty becomes a source of clarity instead of confusion.

Week 1: Assess Current Measurement Quality

- Choose three key metrics you use regularly.
- Conduct reliability testing: measure same athlete three times under identical conditions.
- Calculate typical variation ranges for each metric.
- Establish minimum thresholds for "meaningful change".

Week 2: Practice Probabilistic Language

- Review your last five recommendations to stakeholders.
- Identify where you presented certainties that were actually probabilities.
- Rewrite three recommendations using probability-based language.
- Practice framing uncertainty as professional caution rather than indecision.

Week 3: Evaluate Research Studies

- Find three studies or vendor claims relevant to your work.
- Apply the fifteen-minute review method to each.
- Look for red flags and assess practical significance.
- Document which claims warrant implementation and which warrant skepticism.

Week 4: Implement Decision Frameworks

- Choose one recurring decision you make under uncertainty.
- Apply the **Confidence-Action Framework** to structure your approach.
- Document your reasoning and confidence level.
- Plan follow-up evaluation to assess decision quality.

Quarterly Uncertainty Audit

Every three months, conduct a structured review:

- What were you most confident about that turned out differently than expected?
- Which uncertain situations turned out better than predicted?
- Where could better information have led to different decisions?
- Which uncertainties were worth addressing, and which were distractions?

Include key stakeholders such as coaches, training staff, and athletes whenever possible. Their perspectives often reveal context and consequences that might otherwise go unnoticed. Over time, consistent reflection evolves into an adaptive system that builds confidence, precision, and trust even when certainty is impossible.

From Numbers to Insight

Statistical literacy isn't about becoming a mathematician. It's about developing judgment—knowing when you have enough information to act confidently, when you need more data, and when you should acknowledge uncertainty while still providing useful guidance.

A field hockey coach once said, "I used to think my job was to eliminate uncertainty. Now I realize it's to make the best decisions possible with uncertain information and adjust based on what we learn." That philosophy captures the essence of applied sport science.

Great practitioners share this ability. They read data without worshiping it, trust evidence without pretending it tells the whole story, and adjust quickly when reality proves them wrong. They operate with confidence rooted in process, not perfection.

Clarity about uncertainty also strengthens technology decisions. The most valuable tools don't promise certainty or claim to predict the future. They support better judgment by providing clear, reliable information within context. In the next chapter, we'll explore how to select technology that enhances judgment rather than replaces it.

Effective sport science makes good decisions with imperfect information rather than waiting for perfect data.

 KEY TAKEAWAYS

EMBRACE UNCERTAINTY

- Accept measurement error and variability as unavoidable realities.
- Focus on distinguishing meaningful signals from noise.
- Make decisions confidently with imperfect information by applying probabilistic thinking.

6

CHOOSE TECHNOLOGY THAT FITS

"You have to know what the problem is before you can solve it. Otherwise, you're just guessing."

BILL PARCELLS

Choose Technology That Fits

A PROFESSIONAL SOCCER CLUB introduced GPS tracking vests, but the head coach used the data primarily to call out players who "weren't working hard enough." Over time, players viewed the system as a tool for criticism rather than performance. Tension grew between athletes and staff, and compliance dropped. The decline extended beyond GPS monitoring to other areas of the performance program as trust eroded.

Another club adopted the same GPS system but began by involving players in the rollout. Before collecting data, the sport scientist met with both players and coaches to agree on which metrics would be shared and how they would be used. Reports highlighted both underprepared and overprepared states, helping athletes manage workloads and coaches guide recovery. The process became collaborative instead of punitive. Players began competing to reach high-speed running targets and requesting individual summaries. Compliance stayed near perfect, and the training staff used the data consistently to improve player preparedness.

This contrast captures our fifth Big Rock principle: **Choose Technology That Fits**. Reliability, integration into daily routines, and cultural alignment matter far more than advanced features. The right technology is the one that works every day, fits your environment, and supports real decisions.

The Technology Reality Check

Sport science technology often promises revolutionary performance improvements, but the reality is more complicated. Technology can be extremely valuable, but only when it matches your needs, resources, and culture.

The most successful sport science programs rarely own the most expensive equipment. Instead, they use tools that align with their culture and support high impact decision opportunities. A high school track program with a stopwatch might create more value than a college program with sophisticated but underused timing gates.

Understanding this principle means shifting from asking "What's the latest technology available?" to "What tool will genuinely improve outcomes in our situation?" The most advanced option isn't always the most effective. Choose technology that fits your needs, integrates into your routines, and supports meaningful decisions in your setting.

Start with Problems, Not Solutions

The most common mistake in technology selection happens before any evaluation begins: shopping for solutions without clearly defining the problem. It's like buying medicine before knowing what illness you're treating.

An American football program fell into this trap. After seeing an impressive GPS demo at a conference, they rushed to purchase a full system without first asking what specific question they were trying to answer. The result? Dozens of new metrics appeared, but no clear plan existed for how to use them. Processes slowed down as staff spent time exporting and formatting reports. Coaches grew frustrated when simple questions like "Who looks most fatigued today?" were buried under layers of charts. The system wasn't bad. It just created more noise than clarity because it wasn't tied to a real problem.

Another program started from a different place: a clearly defined need to monitor real-time physiological responses during summer training to prevent heat-related issues. That specific need led them to a simple heart rate monitoring system that fit perfectly. They used it successfully for years because it addressed a real problem they faced every day during summer training.

THE PROBLEM-FIRST TEST

This test ensures you've defined the problem before exploring technology options. Without that clarity, it's easy to get distracted by impressive features that don't tackle your real needs. Before considering any technology, complete this sentence:

> "We need to solve the specific problem of ___ so that we can ___."

If you can't finish this sentence with confidence, you're not ready to evaluate technology.

When Not to Adopt New Technology

Before purchasing anything new, ask yourself:

Can you optimize what you already have? A basketball program was ready to buy a new athlete monitoring platform when they realized they were only using 20% of their current system's features. Six months spent mastering existing tools delivered more value than any new purchase would have.

Is the timing right? Technology adopted during chaos rarely succeeds. A soccer club purchased GPS systems right before a coaching change. The new staff had different priorities, and the unused vests became an expensive storage problem.

Will it distract from higher priorities? If you're still struggling with basic programming or coach-athlete relationships, adding complex technology often makes things worse, not better. Master the fundamentals first.

The default answer should be "not yet." Technology should solve problems, not create them.

The Five Cs Framework

When evaluating technology options, assess each against five critical dimensions (**Figure 20**) that help identify what works best for your environment:

OPTION	CAPABILITY	COMPATIBILITY	COMPLEXITY	COST-EFFECTIVENESS	CONTINUITY	TOTAL SCORE
NO-TECH APPROACH	●●●	●●●●●	●	●●●●●	●●	16
LOW-TECH SOLUTION	●●●	●●●	●●●	●●●●	●●●●●	18
HIGH-TECH SOLUTION	●●●●●	●●●●	●●●●●	●	●	16

The right technology isn't the most advanced.
It's the one that works best for your environment.

Figure 20. *The Five Cs framework: A systematic evaluation tool that scores technology options across capability, compatibility, complexity, cost-effectiveness, and continuity to identify the best fit for your environment.*

1. ***Capability:*** *Does it solve your specific problem effectively?*

Focus on your needs, not on impressive features. A collegiate track program nearly purchased an expensive biomechanical analysis system offering dozens of measurements when they only needed basic sprint technique feedback. A simpler video analysis app provided exactly what they needed at one-tenth the cost, and because it was easy to use, coaches used it daily. If you can't clearly describe how a metric will influence a specific decision, it isn't a capability you need.

Pro tip: Ask vendors to demonstrate how their tool specifically addresses your problems, not just what it can measure. Request independent validation data and talk to current users about real-world reliability.

2. ***Compatibility***: *Will it align with your existing systems and workflows?*

Even the most capable technology fails if it doesn't play nicely with your current approach. A soccer program purchased a player monitoring system that couldn't export data to their existing database. Coaches ended up manually transferring information, creating a workflow nightmare that caused frustration and fatigue.

Pro tip: Map your current workflow before purchasing. Will this tool fit seamlessly, or will it create extra work? Check data access options and ensure compatibility with your other systems from day one.

3. ***Complexity***: *Can your team realistically use it in your environment?*

The most complex tools often promise more, but the simplest reliable option is usually the one teams can use every day.

Pro tip: Pilot the technology with multiple staff members, not just your tech expert. If only one person can operate it, build redundancy or reconsider whether it's worth the dependency.

4. ***Cost-effectiveness***: *Does the total value justify the complete investment?*

Like an iceberg, the price tag is often just the visible tip. Below the surface lurk installation fees, training time, subscriptions, maintenance, and ongoing support needs.

But there is also a subtler layer of cost: the time, energy, and focus your staff must spend learning, troubleshooting, and extracting value from the system. If the tool is too difficult to operate or requires frequent expert support, those hidden burdens can outweigh its benefits.

Reality check: A baseball program thought they were getting a bargain on a $12,000 pitch tracking system until they discovered they needed an additional $18,000 annually for subscriptions, replacement sensors, technical support, and data analysis training. The total cost of ownership was far higher than the initial investment suggested and the staff spent more time fixing issues than making decisions.

Pro tip: Always calculate total cost of ownership before purchase. The true price includes time, training, and attention.

5. ***Continuity***: *Will it meet your needs as requirements evolve?*

Technology isn't a one-time purchase. It's a relationship. A basketball program learned this lesson when their analytics software was discontinued after the startup was acquired. They lost three years of historical data because they hadn't considered portability.

Pro tip: Ask directly about data ownership, exportability, and vendor stability. Will you still have access to your data if you switch systems? Will the company keep improving the product, or will you outgrow it?

PRACTITIONER PERSPECTIVE

Q: In your experience, what are two to three common pitfalls when adopting sport technology, and how do you recommend sport scientists best avoid them?

JO CLUBB, MS

1. *"Chasing novelty over utility: It's easy to get excited by innovation, but that doesn't guarantee usefulness. To avoid this, anchor decisions in athlete and coach needs, not tech features.*
2. *Underestimating the human factor: Adoption often fails because key stakeholders (i.e. coaches, athletes, or support staff) don't find it intuitive or valuable. Early collaboration and pilot testing help identify friction points before full rollout.*
3. *Poor implementation planning: Even good technology can fail without a clear plan for who will manage it, how it will be used, and what success looks like. I recommend careful planning of implementation using the 5W1H approach: Who, What, When, Where, Why and How."*

▶ JO CLUBB
Founder | Global Performance Insights

DAVE TAYLOR, MS

"A frequent pitfall in the adoption of sport technology is underestimating the demands of implementation. Even validated systems may fail to influence practice if they're not thoughtfully integrated into existing workflows. Addressing this requires more than technical deployment—it necessitates collaborative engagement. Involving staff throughout the process, from refining the technology's purpose to co-developing reporting outputs, fosters shared understanding and ownership. This participatory approach enhances perceived relevance and facilitates sustained use. While implementation may be championed by a single practitioner, successful integration depends on distributed responsibility and collective investment across the performance team."

► **DAVE TAYLOR**
Director of Performance | Golden State Warriors

MENTAL MODEL MOMENT

SECOND ORDER THINKING

Key Principle: Don't just consider the immediate effects of a decision—ask, "And then what?" Think through the ripple effects.

Think Beyond the First Order

Many technology adoptions fail not because the tool is bad, but because teams focus only on first order benefits. A system might provide cutting-edge data, but what happens when staff don't have time to operate it daily? What happens when the lone expert leaves? What happens when the data isn't easily linked to decisions?

These downstream consequences often determine success or failure more than the initial capability (**Figure 21**). Effective technology selection means asking not just what a tool can do, but what it will require and change in your unique setting.

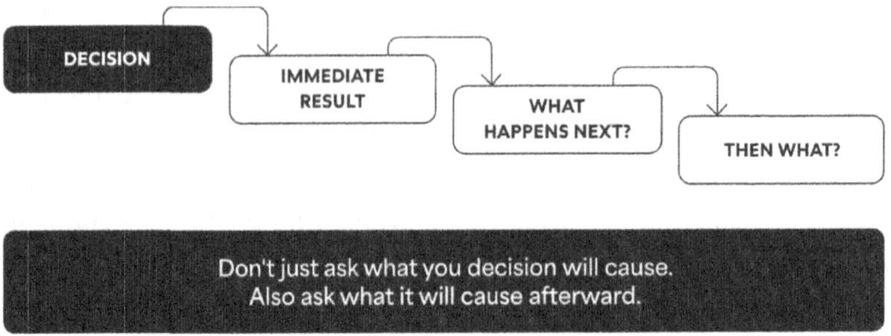

Figure 21. *Second order thinking: Consider both immediate effects and downstream consequences of decisions to avoid unintended problems that emerge later.*

The Technology Spectrum

Not every problem needs a high-tech answer. Often, the best solution is the simplest one. The key is matching the level of technology to your actual needs, resources, and constraints. Three different programs address the same need: monitoring athlete readiness, each using a different point on this spectrum.

No-Tech Approach

Athletes circle numbers on paper forms each morning for sleep quality, soreness, and energy levels. Coaches manually review forms and flag concerning patterns. This system works effectively because it requires no additional resources, fits seamlessly into the daily routine, and provides exactly the information coaches need to adjust training.

Low-Tech Approach

Use Google Forms to collect athlete wellness data each morning, with conditional formatting in Google Sheets automatically highlighting concerning scores and generating a simple summary for coaches. Over time, they can track individual trends, spot recurring issues earlier, and adjust training with greater confidence, all through a process that remains simple to operate and maintain.

High-Tech Approach

A custom athlete-monitoring app with an athlete-facing interface feeds data into an integrated dashboard with automated alerts and historical tracking. The advanced features are justified by the program's resources and the volume of data they manage daily.

All three systems work effectively because they match the organization's needs, resources, and capabilities. The lesson isn't that simpler is always better, but that the right level of technology depends on your particular context.

Practical Technology Selection

Technology can help or hinder depending on how it's chosen. The goal isn't to chase new features, but to match tools to real problems, existing workflows, and available resources. These principles offer a simple guide for making technology choices that last.

Requirements Matrix Method

Create a simple spreadsheet with your requirements as rows and potential technology options as columns. Separate must-have features from nice-to-have capabilities.

A volleyball program used this method when selecting a jump monitoring system. Instead of choosing the most feature-rich option, they identified essential requirements:

- Accurately measures jump height
- Works reliably in their gym environment

- Allows multiple athletes to be tested simultaneously
- Requires minimal setup time
- Additional features such as asymmetry tracking were nice to have but not essential

This systematic approach revealed that the mid-range option met all their essential requirements at a fraction of the cost of premium systems. More importantly, it fit perfectly into their operational constraints, leading to consistent daily use rather than sporadic utilization.

Test Before You Buy

Many technology failures could be prevented by trying systems in real-world conditions before committing to purchase. This doesn't always mean a formal trial. It could mean visiting programs already using the tool or requesting a demonstration in your own environment.

Plan Implementation from Day One

Even the best technology fails if it isn't implemented effectively. Consider:

- Who will champion the technology?
- Who will resist it and why?
- What training will be required?
- What additional resources will you need?
- How will the technology connect with existing workflows?

Successful implementation depends more on people and processes than on the technology itself. Plan for both from day one.

Common Technology Traps

Most technology struggles arise less from the tools themselves and more from how they're chosen and rolled out. The same patterns appear across programs, yet each one is avoidable once you know what to look for.

The Feature Creep Trap

Impressive capabilities often distract teams from what they truly need. It's like buying a Swiss Army knife with fifty tools when you only ever use two. Each extra feature can add layers of complexity, extra cost, and a new way for things to break.

> MENTAL MODEL MOMENT
>
> **INVERSION**
>
> *Key Principle:* Instead of asking "What should we do?" ask "What should we avoid?" Turning a problem upside down often makes the next step obvious.

Inversion thinking becomes powerful here **(Figure 22)**. It's a simple but effective mental model: flip the question. Instead of asking "What technology will help us succeed?", ask "What could make this implementation fail, and why?"

This shift in perspective forces you to look for weaknesses instead of chasing new features. It turns attention toward the barriers such as workload, culture, expertise, or workflow that can quietly derail progress before a tool even gets used. Common failure modes include:

- Choosing technology that requires expertise the staff doesn't have
- Selecting systems that don't fit the facility or bandwidth constraints
- Buying solutions that create more work instead of reducing it
- Implementing tools that nobody wants to use

By mapping out what could cause failure, you build resilience into your selection process and avoid the traps that turn expensive tools into expensive paperweights.

An American football program used this logic through a "weekly use test." For each feature, they asked whether it would be used weekly, monthly, or never. Features outside the weekly category were labeled "nice to have" rather than essential. The process led them to choose a simpler GPS system that met their needs and worked every day without added complexity.

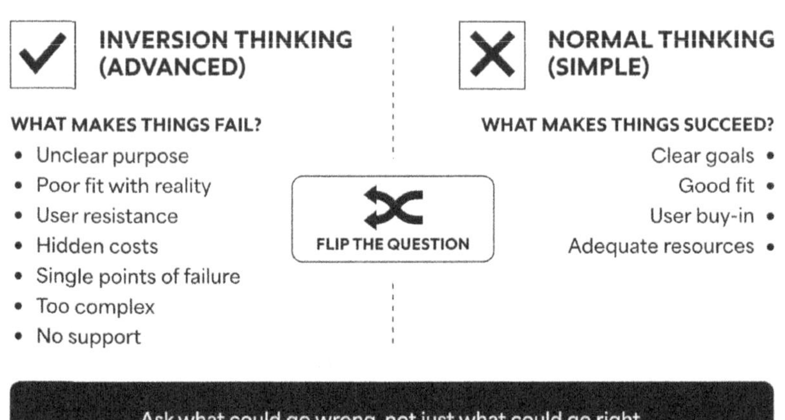

Figure 22. *Inversion thinking: Identifying what could go wrong reveals clearer paths to success than only focusing on what could go right.*

The Demonstration Effect

Technology often performs beautifully in presentations yet falls apart once real life begins. Demonstrations are usually set up under perfect conditions, with ideal data, experienced operators, and unlimited time. Real environments rarely look like that. To avoid this trap:

- Ask for demonstrations in environments that resemble your own
- Speak with programs that have similar resources and constraints.
- Arrange a trial period so you can test the system in your workflow

Evaluating a tool under the same pressures you face daily reveals whether it's built for your world or only for the showroom floor.

The Integration Illusion

Teams often expect new technology to fit smoothly into existing systems. In reality, integration usually requires extra setup, custom connections, and workflow adjustments that aren't obvious at first.

Before committing, verify how data will move between platforms, who will manage those connections, and what happens when updates or system changes occur. Successful integration depends as much on planning and people as it does on the solution itself.

Technology for Different Contexts

No two environments face identical challenges. What works in a professional club may fail in a high school. What succeeds in research may not work well in daily coaching. The examples below show how context shapes technology choices, even when the underlying principles stay the same.

Resource-Limited Environments

Focus on low-maintenance tools that handle core problems without requiring heavy support or complex upkeep. Look for solutions that strengthen existing routines rather than replacing them entirely.

A high school track program built an effective timing system using smartphone apps, a shared spreadsheet, and volunteer athlete timers. It wasn't as advanced as professional systems, but it gave coaches exactly what they needed to track progress and guide training.

Similarly, a college American football program replaced expensive force plates with a $30 jump mat app that athletes could use independently. Coaches got reliable vertical jump data without the setup time or technical expertise force plates required. The lesson? In resource-limited settings, accessibility often matters more than precision.

High-Resource Environments

Greater resources allow for more sophisticated systems, but the programs that thrive focus on defined performance questions instead of collecting data simply because they can.

A professional Australian Rules Football club learned this the hard way. Despite having budget for any system, they found their $200,000 biomechanics lab sat unused because it couldn't be accessed quickly between training sessions. They pivoted to portable field-based video analysis that integrated into daily routines—less impressive on paper, but actually used every day. Money can't buy integration.

Academic and Research Environments

These settings face a unique challenge: balancing research-level precision with practical application. Effective programs clearly separate these functions, using different standards and often different technologies for research and daily athlete monitoring.

Building Competence

Technology is only as strong as the people using it. The real investment lies in your team's ability to evaluate, implement, and apply it effectively. Technology competence involves:

- Awareness of what tools and systems exist
- The ability to critically assess options against needs
- Skills for deploying technology with consistency and confidence
- The capability to connect different tools into a unified system
- Creativity to adapt technology for your unique requirements

Develop technology competence through:

- Cross-training staff on multiple systems
- Designating technology champions for specific tools
- Building basic data literacy across all staff
- Establishing clear documentation for all technology processes
- Scheduling regular skill development sessions

📝 Your Technology Selection Action Plan

Good technology choices don't happen by chance. They come from a structure of intention. This plan turns the chapter's principles into practical steps for selecting tools that will work in your environment.

Week 1: Problem Definition

- Identify one particular problem you face that technology might help solve.
- Complete the **Problem-First Test** sentence clearly.
- Document current workarounds and their limitations.
- Define success criteria: what would "solved" look like?

Week 2: Context Assessment

- Assess your environment using the **Five Cs Framework.**
- Document resource constraints, technical capabilities, and integration requirements.
- Identify everyone who would need to use the technology.
- Map your current workflows and where the tool would fit.

Week 3: Option Evaluation

- Research three to five potential solutions across different technology levels (no-tech to high-tech).
- Create a requirements matrix comparing must-have vs. nice-to-have features.
- Calculate total cost of ownership, including time and training.
- Request demos or trials in settings similar to yours.

Week 4: Implementation Planning

- Select the option that best fits your context using the **Five Cs Framework.**
- Develop a clear implementation timeline with milestones.
- Plan training and communication strategies.
- Establish how you'll measure success once it's in place.

Making Technology Decisions

Smart technology decisions blend structure with common sense. Frameworks help organize your thinking, but judgment determines whether a tool truly fits your environment.

Start by defining the problem you want to solve, then assess your situation with the **Five Cs**: capability, compatibility, complexity, cost-effectiveness, and continuity. The goal isn't perfection—just a balanced fit that meets your essential needs. This clarity prevents costly mistakes.

Technology should strengthen trust and decision-making, not replace them. Both soccer programs in our opening story used the same GPS system, yet one created tension while the other built collaboration. Success came not from the tool but from how well it fit the team's culture and routines.

Choose tools that serve your reality, not your wish list. When technology aligns with your culture and supports clear decisions, it works. When it doesn't, it becomes a daily reminder of poor alignment.

From selecting technology that fits your context, we move to our final challenge: connecting all elements of sport science into integrated workflows that function seamlessly in real-world conditions.

Effective technology selection prioritizes fit with your specific context over impressive capabilities.

KEY TAKEAWAYS

CHOOSE TECHNOLOGY THAT FITS

- Select technology based on solving real problems within your context.
- Evaluate tools using clear criteria for accuracy, efficiency, and actionability.
- Avoid chasing trends and prioritize fit over flash.

7

CONNECT EVERYTHING SEAMLESSLY

"Our success came when we figured out how to blend all the pieces—not just have them."

STEVE KERR

Connect Everything Seamlessly

A PROFESSIONAL BASKETBALL TEAM had all the right pieces: GPS tracking, wellness surveys, video analysis, and performance testing. Each system worked well on its own, yet together they created frustration instead of progress.

Coaches received separate reports from different specialists, often with conflicting recommendations. Practitioners entered similar information into multiple systems. No one had a complete view of athlete status, and important insights slipped through the cracks.

When a new performance director arrived, she didn't add more technology. She connected what already existed. Data from every system flowed into one shared workflow that generated unified daily recommendations. Clear rules resolved conflicting information, and everything centered on the decisions coaches and athletes needed to make.

Within six weeks, confusion turned into coordinated action. Coaches felt informed rather than buried in data. Athletes saw how each metric linked to their development and preparedness. The program shifted from a pile of disjointed tools to a single, functioning system that improved performance.

This transformation illustrates our sixth Big Rock: **Connect Everything Seamlessly**. The Big Rocks are like ingredients in a recipe: each has value, but only when combined in the right way does the final result come together. Cohesive sport science programs don't rely on separate parts; they coordinate every principle into workflows that function seamlessly in real environments.

The Integration Challenge

Most sport science programs evolve naturally. You start by building monitoring systems from your context assessment, create visualizations that drive action, apply uncertainty frameworks, and add technology that supports those steps. Each piece makes sense on its own, yet the collective result often creates complexity instead of clarity.

It's like a kitchen where the refrigerator, stove, sink, and cutting board are in different rooms. Each tool works perfectly, but preparing a meal becomes exhausting because nothing connects. Energy is wasted moving between isolated components instead of cooking.

Integration means designing workflows where each Big Rock contributes to sharper, more confident decisions **(Figure 23)**:

- Context clarifies which decisions matter most and what success looks like.
- Systems gather and organize the right information.
- Visualization and communication turn that information into clear, actionable insight.

- Uncertainty frameworks keep confidence and ranges visible so choices are calibrated, not reactive.
- Technology supports the flow of information between people and processes.

The integration of these components is what makes better-informed decisions possible. Each Big Rock adds value on its own, but connecting them creates the clarity and consistency needed to systematically improve athlete health and performance. True sport science integration is about aligning principles so decisions become more confident, coordinated, and effective across every level of sport.

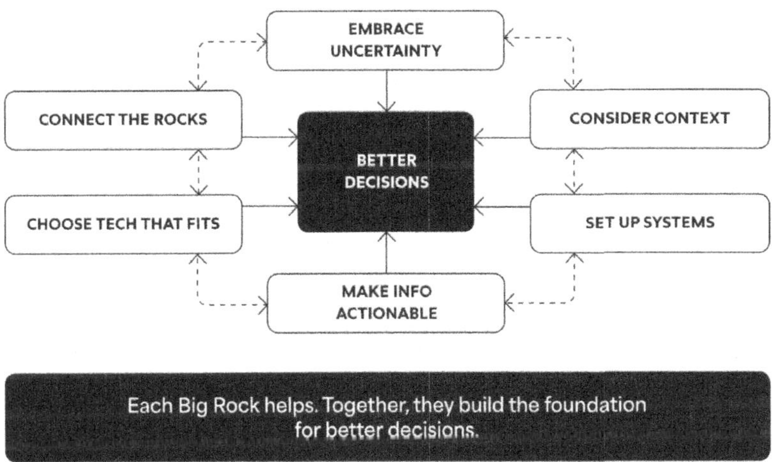

Figure 23. *Big Rocks integration: Each principle connects to and reinforces the others, creating a unified decision-making framework that's stronger than individual components.*

Understanding Decision-Making Workflows

Before you can integrate effectively, you must first understand how decisions happen within your environment. Many practitioners focus on collecting and analyzing data but never map how those activities connect to the decisions they're meant to inform.

A swimming program learned this during an in-season review. They had detailed athlete preparedness and workload reports, but coaches still relied on observation and conversation to plan daily sessions. The problem wasn't data access or quality. It was timing. Information arrived after decisions were already made. When the performance staff mapped the coaches' decision points for how the athletes trained, they found three key moments:

1. Adjusting sets during practice based on how athletes responded
2. Planning next-day sessions in the evening
3. Reviewing overall training direction during weekend staff meetings

To match these rhythms, the performance staff delivered athlete preparedness scores during morning pool setup so coaches could act before practice began. They sent concise workload summaries each evening and provided weekly reports ahead of weekend planning meetings. The data itself stayed the same, but its timing and delivery made it valuable. Once information arrived in sync with real decisions, it finally influenced how training choices were made.

Simple Integration Rules

Integration isn't about cramming all your Big Rocks together at once. It's about connecting them in ways that make decisions easier. These three rules keep integrations simple and practical.

Rule 1: Start with Your Reality

Don't copy what other programs do. Instead, ask: "What decisions do I make?" and "What constraints do I face?" A high school American football program's simple spreadsheet might work better than a professional team's expensive software if it fits their real situation.

Rule 2: Make Information Useful

Don't collect data and hope someone uses it. Deliver it where and when decisions are made. If coaches plan training during lunch conversations, meet them then with insights that inform those plans. If athletes review feedback in the locker room after training, provide it there, when it's most likely to shape what they do next.

Rule 3: Expect Things to Go Wrong

Don't assume your data is perfect. Always have backup plans. When heart rate monitors fail, have simple alternatives ready. When data conflicts, agree on rules for resolving it. When people don't understand, communicate with simpler explanations.

The Integrated Decision Framework

To make consistently informed decisions, you must connect the six Big Rocks into a single workflow. The Integrated Decision Framework provides that structure: a way to move from understanding to action that reflects all six principles. It builds upward from the foundations introduced throughout the book, turning awareness into coordination and coordination into confident, repeatable decisions.

Start with Understanding Context

Every effective decision begins with clarity about what is really happening and why it matters. Before reacting, slow down to define the situation clearly. Identify the problem you're trying to address, the factors shaping it, and the people whose perspectives contribute to the decisions surrounding the problem.

Use the principles from **Chapter 2** to map your environment. Look at schedules, resource limits, and constraints that influence what's possible. Acknowledge how culture, relationships, and timing affect how decisions play out. This isn't background information. It defines the playing field.

Build Systems Around Important Decisions

Once the situation is defined, build structure around it. Use the principles from **Chapter 3** to ensure information naturally supports the choices that matter most by turning awareness into usable processes.

Rather than collecting every possible metric, design workflows that deliver the minimum effective information required to make the most important decisions well. Align what you collect with the real decision points: what gets measured, when it's reviewed, and who acts on it.

At this stage, you're turning insight into infrastructure. The data you gather should directly help solve the problem identified in the previous step and fit the context you operate in. Strong infrastructure doesn't simply store data—it serves decisions.

Make Information Actionable

With systems in place, focus on how information becomes useful. This step builds on the structure you have created by transforming data into understanding. Use the principles from **Chapter 4: Make Information Actionable** to turn information into something that drives behavior.

Simplify how information is presented so the message is unmistakable. Use visuals that highlight patterns and trends instead of overwhelming detail. Add comparisons, such as historical trends, group norms, or thresholds, to give data context and meaning. Design dashboards, reports, and visualizations with a clear communication goal: to make the decision easier for the person using the information.

When information is timely, clear, and relevant, it becomes a shared language. The right people see what matters most, interpret it correctly, and act with confidence. Numbers stop being debated and start driving purposeful action.

Embrace and Quantify Uncertainty

Once information is clear and reaches the right people, the next step is understanding how confident you are in what the information shows. Use the principles from **Chapter 5: Embrace Uncertainty** to interpret the strength of your evidence and scale your actions accordingly.

Recognize that uncertainty isn't a weakness. It's a guide for judgment. When confidence in the data or situation is high, act decisively. When it is low, act proportionally: pause, test, or gather more information before committing fully. Calibrate your responses so decisions reflect both evidence and confidence.

Good practitioners document how sure they are and revisit outcomes later to refine that sense of confidence. Over time, this habit builds trust, accountability, and learning across the organization. It shifts conversations away from who is "right" toward how sure the group should be and what to do next.

Use Technology That Fits the Environment

After context, systems, clarity, and uncertainty are addressed, technology can now enhance decision-making instead of complicating it. Apply the lessons from **Chapter 6: Choose Technology That Fits** to ensure tools match your environment, staff, and workflow.

Select technology that supports the people using it. The goal isn't to have the most advanced system, but the one that integrates smoothly into daily routines. The right tools reduce friction, save time, and help staff act on information faster. Automation should simplify what is predictable while freeing people to focus on interpretation and dialogue.

Technology adds value only when it strengthens connection and trust between those interpreting the data. When it fits your process, it becomes invisible: quietly improving how information moves through your ecosystem.

Connect Everything Seamlessly

Integration happens when all Big Rocks reinforce one another. Context guides what matters. Systems organize information around decisions. Actionable communication ensures clarity. Uncertainty calibrates confidence. Technology supports and connects every layer.

This is where everything comes together. Integration isn't about linking every data feed or using a single software platform. It's about aligning how people think, interpret, and communicate so decisions stay consistent across the organization or environment.

When context, systems, clarity, confidence, and technology align, information turns into collective understanding. Everyone can see the same situation through the same lens and that's what drives coherent, confident, and coordinated action.

The Value of Thought Experiments

Before launching a new process, mentally walk through what could go wrong. Imagine how each stakeholder might respond, what information could be misunderstood, or how systems might fail under pressure. These mental rehearsals expose weak points early and clarify how to adapt before issues appear **(Figure 24)**:

For example, a professional ice hockey performance director preparing to introduce a new monitoring workflow imagined potential pitfalls: what if data uploads failed, or coaches felt the system limited their autonomy? By thinking through these possibilities, she adjusted communication plans and backup protocols in advance to ensure smooth implementation.

Thought experiments are a practical form of foresight. They cost nothing, prevent chaos, and strengthen confidence in the systems you build. The most forward-thinking practitioners don't just design workflows; they also mentally test them before putting them into play. When designing new workflows, experienced practitioners imagine possible outcomes.

MENTAL MODEL MOMENT

THOUGHT EXPERIMENTS

Key Principle: Mentally simulate scenarios to evaluate outcomes and stress-test your decisions without real-world risk.

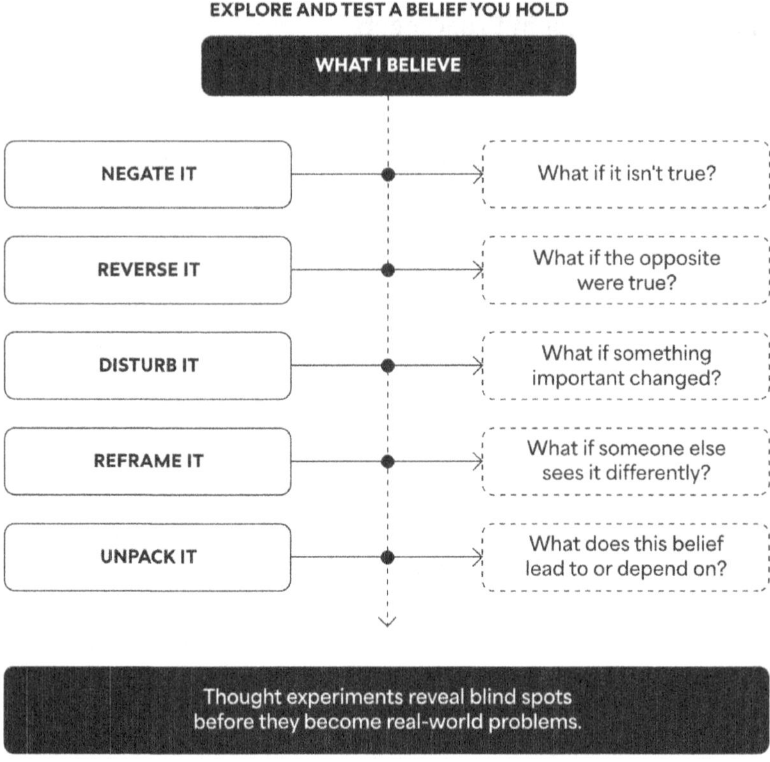

Figure 24. *Thought experiments: Testing beliefs and assumptions through systematic mental simulation reveals potential problems before they occur.*

Coordinating Applied Sport Science

Integration builds the playbook. Coordination runs the plays. Once the Big Rocks are connected, the next step is keeping people, systems, and information working together at the right times. Sport science isn't just about collecting and communicating data. It's about ensuring that the right information reaches the right people when it matters most. Some coordination happens automatically, some requires regular planning, and some demands immediate attention when challenges arise.

Daily Coordination

These are the background processes that keep daily operations running smoothly. A youth soccer program created simple alerts that flagged when an athlete had two poor sleep nights in a row. The goal wasn't to automate decisions. The goal was to prompt quick conversations about whether to adjust training demands or address sleep habits. Consistent awareness helped staff stay proactive and make better daily decisions.

Weekly Coordination

These processes require regular attention but not daily focus. The same soccer program held short Monday meetings where coaches, training staff, and sport scientists reviewed key trends and planned responses for the week ahead. These meetings kept the group aligned, turned last week's lessons into next week's actions, and prevented small problems from turning into big ones.

Crisis Coordination

When early warning signs appear, acting fast prevents bigger problems. In the same soccer program, one athlete reported knee pain while two others logged elevated lower body soreness scores. Because the staff already had a crisis action plan, they immediately met to review workloads, recent surface changes, and strength session volumes. Within hours, they adjusted training intensity and flagged similar risk patterns across the roster. Planning these responses ahead of time kept the process calm and coordinated instead of chaotic and reactive.

Building Trust Through Integration

Information, and the systems that connect it to decisions, only create impact when people trust them. Credibility is the foundation of coordinated sport science. Staff must believe that the information they receive is reliable and genuinely supports better decision-making. Trust doesn't appear overnight; it develops as value is demonstrated consistently over time **(Figure 25)**. Understanding how that trust forms helps you remain patient early and deliberate as relationships strengthen.

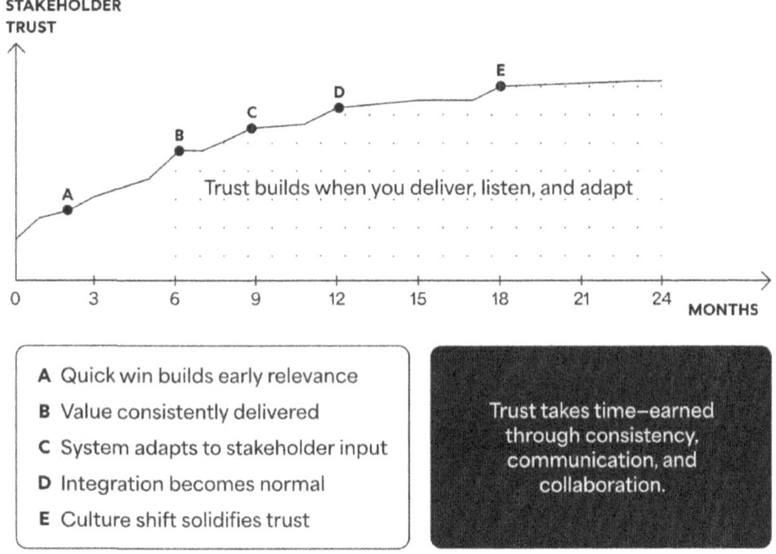

Figure 25. *Stakeholder trust-building timeline: Trust develops predictably through phases of credibility building, value demonstration, adaptation, and cultural integration over 24 months.*

The Trust Development Process

Trust in coordinated sport science systems tends to follow a predictable pattern across most organizations.

Months 1–3 | Establishing Credibility: Skepticism early on is normal. Many coaches and staff have probably seen new systems overpromise and underdeliver. Focus on solving one real problem quickly instead of showing everything you can do.

A college track program built early trust by addressing coaches' biggest frustration: inconsistent information about daily athlete participation plans. Instead of launching a complex monitoring system, they created a simple morning check-in that confirmed each athlete's plan for the day, including class schedules, strength training, and event-specific work. That one reliable improvement built confidence and set the foundation for future progress.

Months 4–6 | Consistent Value Demonstration: Trust accelerates when benefits show up regularly. Share wins, even small ones.

An American football program documented how their workflow may have helped prevent two potential injuries during training camp. Those results gave coaches confidence that the system was working for them, and they asked to keep using it once the season began.

Months 7–12 | Collaboration and Ownership: This stage is about building with people, not just for them. Once early trust is established, invite stakeholders to help refine how the system works. Ask for feedback, involve them in small design decisions, and show how their input shapes updates. When coaches, performance staff, and athletes see their ideas reflected in the process, they become invested in its success. That shared ownership transforms the system from "yours" to "ours," laying the groundwork for long-term buy-in and sustainability.

Months 13–24 | Cultural Integration: At this stage, trust becomes part of the organization's identity. The systems and habits built over the first year evolve into shared expectations that define how things are done, not just who does them. New staff members inherit confidence in the process because it has already proven its worth. The framework no longer depends on individual champions; it sustains itself through collective belief and consistent results.

Trust-Building Strategies

Earning trust isn't about big gestures; it's about small wins delivered consistently. These strategies help maintain credibility and strengthen collaboration as integration expands.

Start Small, Deliver Consistently: Choose one connection point that solves a real problem people face daily. Execute it flawlessly over a sustained period before adding anything new. A swimming program built trust by ensuring training intensity recommendations were always available when coaches needed them. They didn't miss a single day for three months, and that reliability built lasting confidence.

Acknowledge Limitations Honestly: When processes fail or information is uncertain, communicate clearly and take ownership. Coaches and staff respect transparency far more than excuses. Trust grows when people see consistent effort to improve rather than attempts to defend flawed systems.

Involve Stakeholders in Design: The most effective systems are built with people, not for them. Regular feedback sessions where coaches, athletes, and support staff shape how data is used create ownership and shared investment. When stakeholders help design workflows, they also protect and sustain them.

Connection Point Management

Trust can erode quickly when information breaks down between people or systems. The most vulnerable areas of any workflow are the connection points, where information moves from one process, person, or platform to another. Managing these transitions deliberately keeps integration reliable.

Information Handoffs

Ever played the game of telephone? Someone whispers a message to the next person, who passes it along again, and by the time the message reaches the last person, it sounds nothing like the original. Information in sport science can work the same way if you're not careful. Each time data moves between people or systems, details can get lost or distorted.

A college strength and conditioning staff once shared performance data with coaches through a long text thread. After several added comments, the original message had been interpreted three different ways and key context was missing. The strength and conditioning staff solved the issue by creating a shared dashboard that displayed the same summary for everyone. Clear, direct handoffs preserved the message and kept everyone on the same page.

Decision Escalation Pathways

Not every alert needs the same response. Some issues resolve automatically, while others demand human judgment and action. Establish clear thresholds for when responsibility shifts from systems to staff. For example, if two risk indicators trigger together, the performance and medical teams review the surrounding information within two hours. Clear escalation rules keep everyone accountable, prevent overreactions to minor alerts, and stop important situations from slipping through the cracks.

Sustaining Integration Over Time

Integration isn't a finish line. It is an ongoing process that needs regular attention to stay functional and relevant. Contexts change, technology updates, and staff come and go. Keeping your systems connected requires deliberate maintenance, consistent feedback, and planned adaptation

Regular System Health Checks

Set aside time each month to evaluate how well your systems and processes communicate. Don't just confirm that individual tools are working. Follow how information moves from collection to decision. A gymnastics program conducted monthly "information flow audits," tracing a single decision from data entry to final action. Each audit revealed where handoffs slowed down or context was lost, allowing small fixes before they became bigger problems.

Stakeholder Feedback Loops

The people using your systems are the best source of insight into whether your process is actually working. Create simple, regular ways for coaches, athletes, and staff to share what helps, what confuses, and what slows them down. A professional basketball sport science department collected short feedback from coaches and performance staff after each new report or workflow update, then used that input to refine how information was presented in the next iteration. The routine took less than five minutes but made staff feel heard and kept the system improving.

Adaptation Protocols

Even well-designed systems need to evolve. Plan ahead for how your workflows will adapt when tools, people, or priorities change. Treat updates as part of the process, not interruptions. A professional soccer program prepared for this by outlining how each major system upgrade, such as a new video analysis platform or updated database, would connect back into existing training and planning workflows. Because the plan was clear, transitions happened smoothly and daily operations never stalled.

Common Integration Pitfalls

Bringing systems together sounds like progress, but not all integration is helpful. Many programs stumble because they confuse complexity with effectiveness, treat technology as the solution itself, or remove the human judgment that gives integration its real value. Recognizing these common pitfalls makes it easier to build systems that are both functional and sustainable. What follows are the most frequent ways integration efforts go wrong, and how to avoid them.

The Complexity Trap

Organizations often assume that sophisticated integration requires complex solutions. The most effective integration often emerges from elegantly simple approaches that connect essential elements without unnecessary complexity. Start with first principles thinking: identify what problem you're solving, what information truly matters, and what the simplest path to action looks like. Once you build an effective and reliable foundation, add complexity only when it provides clear and necessary value.

The Technology Solution Fallacy

Technology can facilitate integration, but it can't create integration. The most robust integration platforms fail if they don't align with decision-making workflows and stakeholder needs. Before building or buying tools, connect with stakeholders to understand the key decisions they make and how they prefer to communicate. Design your systems to support those processes rather than forcing people to adapt to technology.

The Automation Problem

When too much is automated, decisions lose the depth that comes from shared human judgment. The multiple perspectives principle, introduced earlier with the elephant parable, reminds us that the best outcomes come from voices combining, not from automation replacing them. Spark dialogue between groups with different perspectives. The athlete knows how they feel, the coach sees performance trends, the training staff recognize risk. Integration should create conversations that connect these perspectives so decisions reflect the full picture.

PRACTITIONER PERSPECTIVE

Q: What strategies have you used to create a "shared vision" for how to leverage data to support multidisciplinary collaboration between various key stakeholders?

JOHN WAGLE, PhD

"I've found that creating a shared vision for data use starts by reframing it as a tool for alignment and collaboration—not just analysis. It begins with listening: understanding what performance means across coaches, medical staff, front office, and athletes. From there, I focus on co-creating frameworks where data builds trust and enables a shared language around decision-making. By making data clear, visual, and consistent, we reinforce collective understanding and move from siloed inputs to integrated systems—where each stakeholder sees data as a means to drive both individual and team success."

> **JOHN WAGLE**
>
> Senior Associate Athletics Director of Sports Performance | University of Notre Dame

JOSH NELSON, EdD

"Creating and deploying a shared vision is both challenging and fulfilling. Regardless of the content area or discipline, a shared vision begins with a model or ideology that's commonly accepted by stakeholders within the organization.

From personal experience within the athletic performance space, I think a foundational element is to keep athletes at the center of the mission. By keeping the athlete as the focal point, and as active participants in the deployment of the mission, we keep the main thing the main thing in all decision-making. Next, prioritizing active communication across all areas of the organization is key toward facilitating a unified mission. Clear and proactive communication regardless of role ensures that everyone feels heard and that key information is actively scaled from strategic to operational stakeholders. Third, planning and ongoing assessment is key. Both long- and short-term planning around the organizational mission and then routine assessment that the mission/vision is being deployed accurately ensures everyone is going in the right direction. Finally, building a learning organization that grows from experiences and from data collected along the way can galvanize the mission and strengthen the entire group, as a whole."

► **JOSH NELSON**

Director of Performance Science | Atlanta Falcons

Your Integration Action Plan

Integration is like following directions to a new place. You take one turn at a time, not all at once. This plan helps you build integration gradually so that your systems, people, and decisions connect without confusion or unnecessary complexity.

Week 1: Start Simple

- Choose one decision you make regularly, such as adjusting daily training recommendations.
- Write down exactly how you make this decision and what information you rely on.
- Identify which of your Big Rocks could improve the decision if connected.
- Document the current workflow.

Goal: Understand how your current decisions happen before trying to improve them.

Week 2: Connect Two Things

- Take that same decision and link two of your Big Rocks.
- Use your context assessment to adjust how you interpret your system data or combine your performance information with an uncertainty check to guide how strongly to act.
- Test this connection for one week and record what changes.

Goal: Experience the power of a single meaningful connection.

Week 3: Test and Adjust

- Use your new integrated approach for another week.
- Ask yourself whether it makes decisions easier or harder.
- Check if the right people understand it and find it useful.
- Refine your process based on what happens.

Goal: Strengthen what works and simplify what doesn't.

Week 4: Expand One Integration Point

Once your first integration works reliably, expand it.

- Add technology that automates part of your workflow.
- Refine how you visualize or communicate insights.
- Connect another stakeholder group to the process.
- Test each addition for at least a week before expanding further.

Goal: Build upward from stability, not speed.

Month 2 and Beyond: Gradual Expansion

- Every few weeks, add another connection between your Big Rocks.
- Evaluate after each addition to confirm that the process remains simple, fast, and aligned.
- If decisions become harder or clarity decreases, pause and reassess before adding more.

Goal: Integration should make your decisions smoother, not more complicated.

Integration Success Stories

High School Wrestling Program

- **Context**: A high school wrestling team struggled with unhealthy weight-cutting habits and inconsistent communication between athletes, parents, and coaches. Practices varied widely, and safety concerns were rising.
- **System**: The staff built a simple monitoring system centered on daily weigh-ins and athlete check-ins. These were tracked in a shared spreadsheet that automatically updated a color-coded status for each athlete.
- **Actionable Information**: The color indicators (blue, grey, red) summarized athlete preparedness and weight-change at a glance. Coaches could see when patterns were trending toward

risk and start proactive conversations instead of reacting to missed targets.

- **Uncertainty**: To avoid overreacting to day-to-day fluctuations, the staff created safety thresholds based on three-day rolling averages. This approach balanced immediate awareness with confidence in trends over time.
- **Technology**: A mobile app allowed athletes to log their morning weights and self-assessments directly, while parents automatically received updates when their child's status changed.
- **Integration**: The combination of context understanding, simple systems, clear communication, and uncertainty management created an environment of shared accountability.
- **Result**: Dangerous weight cuts dropped significantly, competitive performance remained stable, and trust between families and staff strengthened. The program no longer managed risk reactively. It prevented it through connection and clarity.

Professional Soccer Team

- **Context**: A professional soccer club faced congested match schedules that led to load spikes and potential increases in injury risk. Different departments, including coaching, performance, and medical, interpreted data in isolation, creating confusion.
- **System**: The performance team restructured how load data was stored and shared. Instead of maintaining multiple spreadsheets, they used one central dashboard that summarized key load-based competition preparedness metrics for each player.
- **Actionable Information**: The dashboard highlighted patterns rather than raw numbers, grouping players into preparedness tiers (high, moderate, low) using visual cues that compared each player to their normal range and competition demands.
- **Uncertainty**: Each preparedness tier included a confidence score based on data completeness and recency. These confidence scores guided conversations and shaped the scale of potential actions.

- **Technology:** The new system unified player load, in-game statistics, and medical data into one visualization platform that automatically refreshed daily. Coaches could access it on their tablets whenever needed.
- **Integration:** Daily 10-minute cross-department meetings became standard practice. These brief check-ins aligned context, data, and confidence before every training session.
- **Result**: Players trained more consistently, soft-tissue injuries during congested weeks decreased, and the staff reported higher confidence in workload adjustments. Integration didn't make their system more complex. It made it more connected.

Why These Integrations Worked

Both programs succeeded because they built their decisions on the full foundation of the Big Rocks. They didn't stop at data collection or technology adoption. They began with context, created systems that served important decisions, made information clear, quantified uncertainty, and chose technology that integrated seamlessly into their environment. Integration turned information into shared understanding, and shared understanding into confident action.

Evaluating Integration Effectiveness

Integration is a living process that requires constant evaluation, reflection, and refinement. The best systems evolve as people, environments, and priorities change. To understand how well your integration is working, look for clear signs of progress in how people think, communicate, and act.

Decision Quality Improves

Stakeholders make decisions with greater confidence and clarity. They can describe how coordinated information shapes their choices and use evidence to justify adjustments.

Workflow Friction Decreases

Information moves easily from collection to action. There is less manual effort, fewer misunderstandings, and a clear path from insight to implementation. Staff spend less time managing data and more time applying it.

Stakeholder Engagement Increases

Coaches, athletes, and support staff value the system because it helps them. They use it willingly and consistently rather than working around it.

Adaptation Capability Strengthens

When conditions change, such as injuries, travel, schedule disruptions, or staffing transitions, the system adapts. Integration builds flexibility, not fragility.

Outcomes Demonstrate Value

Integrated decision-making leads to visible results: smoother, better-informed, and more holistic processes. The system proves its worth not through complexity, but through consistency.

The Competitive Advantage of Integration

When your Big Rocks work together, you create capabilities that are difficult for others to copy. Technology can be purchased and personnel can be hired, but integration emerges only through shared understanding, clear communication, and systematic thinking built over time. Other organizations can replicate your tools, but not your connected culture. True competitive advantage grows from alignment—when context, systems, clarity, confidence, and technology reinforce one another through daily habits and shared purpose.

The most successful programs rarely have the most advanced technology. They have the most consistent execution of sound principles within their specific environment. They use data to connect, not to impress. They create workflows that strengthen trust, improve decisions, and sustain performance.

From mastering each Big Rock to connecting them seamlessly, you now hold the complete framework for effective sport science practice. The next step is to keep refining it, evolving with your environment while staying anchored to the principles that make it work.

Effective sport science isn't defined by tools or trends. It's defined by integration: people, systems, and information working together with clarity and confidence.

 KEY TAKEAWAYS

CONNECT EVERYTHING SEAMLESSLY

- Integrate systems so information flows smoothly between people and processes.
- Use simple frameworks to align data collection with decision-making needs.
- Regularly evaluate integration to maintain clarity, relevance, and effectiveness.

CONCLUSION

YOUR SPORT SCIENCE JOURNEY

"You don't rise to the level of your goals. You fall to the level of your systems."

JAMES CLEAR

THE ONE-MILLION-DOLLAR ANSWER

REMEMBER THE QUESTION THAT STARTED OUR JOURNEY TOGETHER: "What would you buy if you had one million dollars to improve athletic performance?"

By now, you know the answer isn't found in any equipment catalog. The one-million-dollar answer is mastering the six Big Rocks that create the foundation for everything else: understanding your context, building systems that work, making information actionable, embracing uncertainty, choosing technology that fits, and connecting everything seamlessly **(Figure 26)**.

You've seen how Coach Martinez revolutionized his wrestling program with $347 worth of simple tools, while expensive technology sat unused in other programs. You've learned why Sarah's basketball monitoring system outperformed complex setups that impressed visitors but frustrated users. You've discovered that resources and technology can support high-level sport science, but they don't guarantee it. Success comes from how clearly you think and how deliberately you apply these principles within your environment.

Figure 26. *The one-million-dollar answer: Mastering the six Big Rocks creates more value than expensive equipment by building integrated decision-making capabilities.*

What You Have Accomplished

You have now developed something far more valuable than familiarity with the latest technology or knowledge of advanced techniques. You have mastered the thinking patterns that separate effective practitioners from those who struggle despite impressive credentials and expensive equipment.

You Understand Your Context (Big Rock #1): You know that the same approach can succeed brilliantly in one environment and fail spectacularly in another. You can honestly assess your resources, culture, competitive environment, and operational realities. Crucially, you understand that constraints aren't limitations. They're design parameters that guide you toward solutions others can't easily copy.

You Build Systems That Actually Work (Big Rock #2): You know the difference between systems designed to impress and systems designed to inform. You start with the decisions you need to make, not the data you can collect. You understand that sustainability matters more than sophistication, and that the best system is the one that gets used consistently.

You Make Information Actionable (Big Rock #3): You transform data into clear guidance that enables better decisions. You design visualizations that drive specific actions rather than just displaying information. You understand that different stakeholders need different information presented in different ways, and you facilitate conversations where data insights combine with human expertise.

You Embrace Uncertainty (Big Rock #4): You make good decisions with imperfect information rather than waiting for perfect data. You think in probabilities, not certainties. You communicate uncertainty as appropriate professional caution rather than indecision, and you're comfortable knowing that good decisions may still lead to poor outcomes, while poor decisions sometimes lead to good ones.

You Choose Technology That Fits (Big Rock #5): You start with clearly defined problems rather than shopping for impressive solutions. You assess technology honestly across capability, compatibility, complexity, cost-effectiveness, and continuity. You understand that technology should enhance human judgment rather than replace it, and you know that the simplest solution that meets your needs is often the best choice.

You Connect Everything Seamlessly (Big Rock #6): You create integrated decision-making workflows where all the Big Rocks reinforce each other naturally. You focus on high-value connection points rather than comprehensive automation. You understand that integration enhances human judgment and makes your sport science practice more than the sum of its parts.

Most importantly, you think differently about sport science challenges. Instead of asking "What is the most advanced technology we can afford?" you now ask "What is the simplest approach that solves our most important problem?" This shift in thinking, from advanced tools to clear thinking, will serve you throughout your career, regardless of how resources, technology, or contexts change around you.

Your Competitive Advantage

The sport science field is full of practitioners chasing the latest trends, copying what successful programs appear to be doing, and implementing solutions without understanding the problems they're meant to solve. They chase the newest metrics and shiniest tools, then wonder why decisions don't improve.

You now understand that effectiveness comes from clear thinking applied consistently, not from sophisticated tools applied sporadically. This gives you a tremendous advantage. While others debate which force plate system to buy, you'll be solving real problems with approaches that suit your context. While others struggle to get stakeholders to use their impressive dashboards, you'll be creating information that people actually want and need. While others overlook the uncertainty within their data and therefore in their interpretations and decisions, you'll be evaluating that uncertainty and using it to strengthen your decision-making frameworks.

You're prepared to create sport science programs that consistently improve athletic performance because you understand that the connections between components matter more than the sophistication of individual parts.

The Path Forward

Your sport science journey is just beginning. The principles in this handbook provide your compass, but the path you take will be uniquely yours. Your context, constraints, athletes, and organizational culture will shape how you apply these Big Rocks in ways that others can't easily copy.

Start Simple

Choose one principle and master it in your specific situation before adding complexity. Resist the temptation to implement everything at once; practitioners who try to do everything at the same time often end up doing many things poorly instead of doing one thing exceptionally well.

Your first priority should be conducting an honest context assessment. Understand your resources, culture, competitive environment, and daily realities. This foundation makes everything else possible.

Then build one system that works in your setting. Focus on a single decision you make regularly and create a reliable way to inform that decision better. Make it simple, sustainable, and valuable to stakeholders. Get this right before adding anything else.

Apply the Mental Models

Throughout this handbook, you've learned nine mental models that can help guide your thinking:

- **The Map Is Not the Territory**: Your data is a simplified representation of reality. Always verify it with context, observation, and athlete feedback.
- **First Principles Thinking**: Break problems down to their fundamentals instead of copying what others do. Ask, "What is the most direct path to our outcome given our constraints?"
- **Circle of Competence**: Know what you understand well and what you don't. Use data to enhance expertise, not replace it.

- **Hanlon's Razor**: When stakeholders resist, assume miscommunication or overload before assuming bad intent. Fix communication first.
- **Occam's Razor**: Choose the simplest solution that works. More complexity doesn't mean better results.
- **Probabilistic Thinking**: Think in probabilities, not certainties. Good decisions can lead to bad outcomes, and that's okay.
- **Second Order Thinking**: Ask "And then what?" Consider the ripple effects of your choices before implementing them.
- **Inversion**: Ask "What should we avoid?" alongside "What should we do?" Preventing mistakes is often more powerful than chasing perfection.
- **Thought Experiments**: Mentally simulate scenarios to test your approaches before applying them in the real world.

These models help you navigate complexity, anticipate challenges, and make better decisions across all stages of your career.

Build for the Long Term

Sport science isn't a destination. It's an ongoing process of learning, adaptation, and improvement. The fields that shape our work will continue to evolve, as will the contexts where we apply them. The most successful practitioners embrace this evolution. They maintain strong foundations built on the Big Rocks while staying open to new ideas, technologies, and methods. They recognize that growth is rarely linear; it unfolds in cycles of clarity and confusion, success and setback.

You'll revisit familiar challenges at deeper levels of understanding as your experience grows. Treat these cycles as opportunities to refine your craft, not as signs of failure.

Remember the Human Element

Sport science is ultimately about people. Behind every data point is an athlete with unique needs, challenges, and goals. The technologies and methods you use are simply tools to help you understand and support them more effectively.

At its best, sport science isn't something you do to athletes; it's something you do with them. It's a collaborative process that values coaches' expertise, athletes' intuition, and staff experience. Your role is to strengthen these human relationships, not replace them with data. The true measure of success isn't the sophistication of your systems or the impressiveness of your technology. It's whether athletes perform better, stay healthier, and develop more effectively because of the decisions you help guide.

PRACTITIONER PERSPECTIVE

Q: How do you personally approach ongoing learning and growth to stay effective and relevant as a sports scientist in a rapidly evolving field?

JOHN WAGLE, PhD

"I approach ongoing learning with the same curiosity and urgency for growth that I expect from the athletes and staff I work alongside. I actively seek out productive collisions between disciplines—intentionally drawing from less obvious domains to challenge assumptions and reframe problems. Through emerging research, conversations with thought leaders, and exposure to environments beyond sport, I look for ideas that can be adapted to create meaningful impact in our setting. I also apply a learning-through-doing mindset, treating our systems and workflows as living labs. For me, staying relevant isn't about accumulating knowledge. It is about translating insight into flexible, athlete-centered solutions that meet the demands of varying contexts."

▶ **JOHN WAGLE**

Senior Associate Athletics Director of Sports Performance | University of Notre Dame

JOSH NELSON, EdD

"I've personally found that a consistent and ongoing approach toward learning works best for me. As opposed to formal blocks in the yearly calendar allocated toward learning, I tend to like to dedicate time each day and week toward informal learning opportunities. These experiences could be as simple as reflecting on my day with an after-action review or engagement in an online course or study for a certification. I tend to also do much better when my learning is planned and project based. For example, if I am exploring a new testing protocol or training methodology, I like to immerse myself in the topic and actively create or teach something. I feel as though when I can actively teach concepts to other staff or athletes, I have a firm grasp on the content and can make it actionable. It essentially becomes a personal learning life cycle: problem to learning to producing and teaching others."

▶ **JOSH NELSON**
Director of Performance Science | Atlanta Falcons

MATT RHEA, PhD

"Given that sport science seems to be one of the fastest evolving areas in the industry, I think it's vital to constantly learn and evolve. My personal approach: read at least 30 minutes every day. I am always reading one book related to sports and one from an unrelated area. I have four Google Scholar searches set to deliver results once per month on a revolving weekly schedule. I read at least three of the articles in their entirety. I like LinkedIn posts from a select list of valued connections and will consistently spend some time scanning posts from people that think very differently than I do. Lastly, once per month I break down one method, habit, or idea that I am extremely confident in with the goal of convincing myself that it is flawed. If I succeed, I move on to something better. The key is consistency, open mindedness, and critical thinking."

▶ **MATT RHEA**
Founder | Rhea Performance Systems

Your First Ninety Days

Here is a practical roadmap for implementing what you've learned (**Figure 27**):

Days 1–30: Foundation Building

- Complete thorough context assessment using the frameworks from **Chapter 2.**
- Identify one specific decision you make regularly that could benefit from better information.
- Apply the **Problem-First Test** from **Chapter 6** to define what information would help.
- Choose the simplest approach that could improve this decision.

Days 31–60: System Implementation

- Build your minimum viable system using principles from **Chapter 3.**
- Focus on sustainability over sophistication.
- Get stakeholder buy-in by demonstrating early value.
- Document what works and what doesn't.

Days 61–90: Integration and Refinement

- Make your information actionable using frameworks from **Chapter 4.**
- Practice communicating uncertainty professionally using **Chapter 5** principles.
- Evaluate any technology needs using the **Five Cs Framework** from **Chapter 6.**
- Begin connecting your approach with other decisions using **Chapter 7** integration strategies.

Beyond 90 Days: Continuous Development

- Add complexity only after simpler approaches prove successful.
- Regularly audit your systems to ensure they remain valuable.
- Adapt your approaches as your context evolves.
- Share your lessons learned with other practitioners.

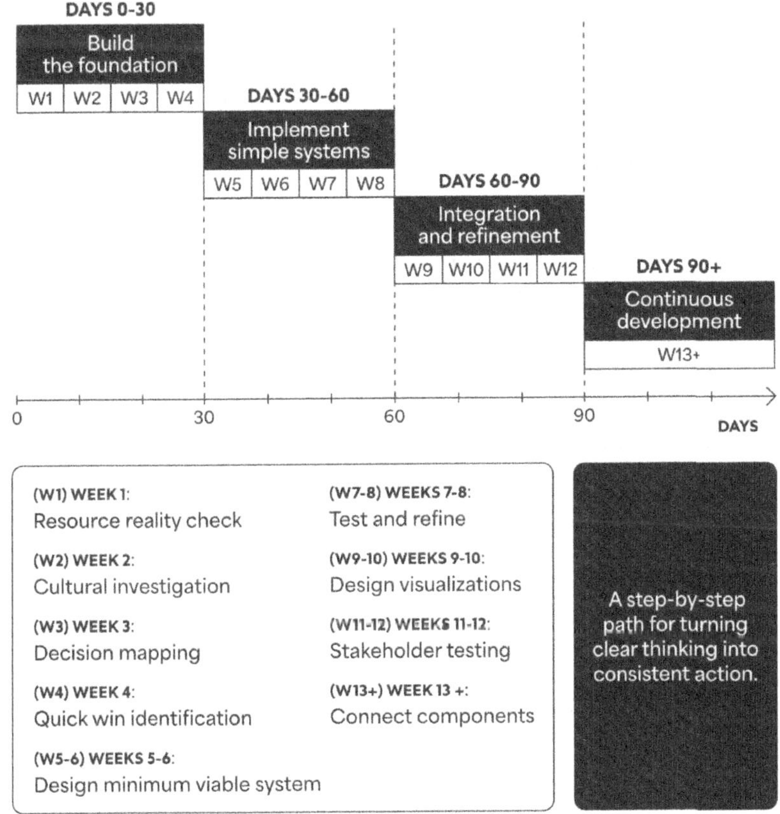

Figure 27. *90-day implementation roadmap: A structured timeline for building sport science capabilities from foundation assessment through system integration and continuous development.*

The Ripple Effect

As you apply these principles consistently, you'll create ripple effects that extend far beyond your immediate work:

Athletes will perform better and stay healthier because you're making smarter decisions about their development and care.

Coaches will feel supported rather than overwhelmed because you provide information they can actually use.

Programs will become more effective and sustainable because they're built on sound principles.

The field will progress as more practitioners focus on clear thinking and practical application rather than technology for its own sake.

Final Thoughts

The athletes you serve deserve nothing less than your best thinking applied consistently in their pursuit of greatness.

The wrestling coach with his $347 weight management system proved that resources don't determine success. He understood his constraints, defined his purpose, and applied sound principles systematically. No perfect conditions. No expensive equipment. Just a clear framework for making decisions within his reality.

You can do the same.

Your situation will be different. Your resources, athletes, and culture are unique. But the principles remain universal. Master the Big Rocks, connect them seamlessly, and you'll build a sport science practice that consistently improves performance while adapting to new challenges.

You'll face skeptical coaches, limited resources, and unexpected setbacks. Good. Constraints aren't obstacles. They're design parameters that force you to focus on what actually matters.

Start where you are. Understand your context. Define your decisions. Build systems that fit your reality.

Sport science succeeds when it fits the reality of your environment. Better thinking leads to better choices. Better choices lead to healthier, higher-performing athletes.

Remember this: the real edge isn't in the data. It's in the decisions it inspires.

Better decisions come from sound principles applied consistently within your constraints.

 KEY TAKEAWAYS

CONCLUSION

- Effective sport science requires thinking clearly and acting purposefully.
- Align systems, tools, and communication with your unique environment.
- Consistently focus on making better decisions that improve athlete outcomes.

Sport science succeeds when it fits the reality of your environment. Clear thinking and purposeful action turn knowledge into better choices. Better choices lead to healthier, higher-performing athletes. The real edge isn't in the data, but in the decisions it inspires.

IN A NUTSHELL

Sport science isn't about having the most tech or the largest datasets. It is about making better decisions consistently. The six **Big Rocks** lay the foundation for effective sport science practice in every environment.

UNDERSTAND YOUR CONTEXT

Before choosing tools or metrics, get clear on your environment, resources, constraints, and stakeholders. Fit always beats flash.

BUILD SYSTEMS THAT ACTUALLY WORK

Design systems that are simple, sustainable, and aligned with real decision-making. Fancy doesn't mean functional.

MAKE INFORMATION ACTIONABLE

Collect only what drives action. Communicate clearly. If the data doesn't inform a decision, it is just noise.

EMBRACE UNCERTAINTY

Perfect information is a myth. Think in probabilities, expect variation, and make confident decisions with imperfect data.

CHOOSE TECHNOLOGY THAT FITS

Start with your problem, not the solution. The best tech is what helps you solve your most important challenge.

CONNECT EVERYTHING SEAMLESSLY

Integrate all Big Rocks into unified workflows. Great sport science connects people and decisions, not just platforms.

ACKNOWLEDGMENTS

We want to thank the athletes, coaches, mentors, colleagues, and friends who challenged our thinking, asked hard questions, and shared their experiences so generously. Every idea here reflects those conversations and collaborations.

We especially thank the practitioners who provided candid feedback on early drafts, helping us make this handbook more useful—especially Dr. Joe Eisenmann and Dr. Jeremy Sibold. Your insights kept us grounded in the realities of the field.

We are also indebted to the practitioners who shared their perspectives in these pages: Dr. Matt Jordan, Sam Contorno, Emma Beanland, Dr. Harjiv Singh, Dr. Dave Tenney, Anna Cruse, Dr. Johann Windt, Dominic Samangy, Daniel Yu, Dr. Patrick Ward, Dr. Ernie Rimer, Dr. Jenny Strickler, Jo Clubb, Dave Taylor, Dr. John Wagle, Dr. Josh Nelson, and Dr. Matt Rhea. Your contributions enriched this work immeasurably.

Finally, to our families—thank you for your patience, support, and understanding throughout the writing process. Your encouragement made this possible.

This handbook is the product of years of shared learning and collaboration with people dedicated to helping athletes thrive. We hope it repays that generosity by providing something practical and meaningful in return.

DEDICATIONS

From Adam:

To Dr. Declan Connolly: professor, colleague, mentor, and friend. You were the spark for this book. What began as an attempt to capture your purpose-driven, practical approach to sport science became my way of honoring how you taught me to think—not just about data, but about people. Though you're no longer with us, your example continues to guide how I approach this field.

To Meghan and Mika: my greatest teammates. Thank you for your patience, love, and constant support through the countless hours it took to bring this book to life.

From Marc:

To Sharlene Elliott: a motherly figure throughout my life. Despite struggling with health issues and the death of your husband, you were a constant presence in my life. As a young man who didn't have parents, was homeless as a teenager, and completed a GED to enter the military, you believed in me and my dreams when no one else did. At times in my life, you were all I had. To you, I am forever grateful.

From both of us:

To our performance family: including coaches, practitioners, athletes, mentors, and educators—those we've worked with, shared ideas with, and who have supported us along the way. The way we think about sport science and human performance has been shaped by each of you. Our writing, our work, and ultimately, our contributions to this field are influenced by you.

MORE RESOURCES
THE SPORT SCIENCE NETWORK

The mission of **The Sport Science Network** is to connect everyone invested in sport—from grassroots coaches to experienced practitioners—by making sport science clearer, more actionable, and more impactful for athletes at all levels.

We connect:

Science to practice.
Information to better decisions.
Knowledge to action.
People to people.
You to practical solutions.

Continue your sport science journey with additional resources, connections, and practical guidance.

sportsciencenetwork.com

ABOUT THE AUTHORS

ADAM VIRGILE, MS

Adam Virgile is an applied sport scientist and researcher with experience across the NBA, NHL, collegiate athletics, and beyond. He has consulted with a wide range of environments—from professional teams in multiple sports to private training facilities and technology companies—helping practitioners build systems that work in their unique contexts. Adam specializes in translating complex physiological and performance information into clear, actionable strategies that empower coaches, athletes, and organizations to make informed decisions at every level of sport.

MARC LEWIS, PhD

Marc Lewis is an applied sport and performance scientist with a variety of experiences in high-performance settings. With academic training in exercise physiology, statistics, and research methodology, he uses his educational background paired with his "in the trenches" experiences to identify problems and find solutions through connecting science with practical application. Marc specializes in working collaboratively to develop and implement effective systems that are solution-oriented and facilitate decision-making processes in highly stressful, chaotic, and time-restricted environments.

Made in the USA
Coppell, TX
15 February 2026

71348072R10098